THE
EXPATRIATE'S
Handbook

THE
EXPATRIATE'S
Handbook

Getting the Best out of Overseas Employment

Bill Twinn • Patrick Burns

KOGAN
PAGE

First published in 1993

Kogan Page Limited
120 Pentonville Road
London N1 9JN

British Library Cataloguing in Publication Data

A CIP record for this book is available from the British Library.

ISBN 0 7494 0899 5

Typeset by Saxon Graphics Ltd, Derby
Printed and bound in Great Britain by Clays Ltd, St Ives plc

Contents

Note: Use of gender

In this text we have usually referred to the expatriate as 'he' and thrown in phrases like 'his family'. This is clearly unsatisfactory for any but the most chauvinist as there are an increasing number of female expatriates doing an excellent job for their companies all over the world. The gender use is therefore entirely a matter of style – referring to 'he or she' all the time is clumsy and using 'one' smacks of a high-class finishing school. The expatriate can be of either sex and, ergo, so can the spouse.

1. Introduction

There have always been expatriates throughout recorded history – people who have migrated searching for economic opportunities with varying degrees of success. The Romans imported their gladiators to thrill the crowds of Rome. During the Middle Ages, whole armies of craftsmen moved around Europe building cathedrals and castles.

It was the colonial period that formalized the modern concept of 'the expatriate' – someone with special skills who ventured overseas to make a fortune. The East India Company represents the typical organization run by expatriates to develop trade in India and this was followed by many more such enterprises in Africa and the Far East. Lonrho, Jardines, Inchcape and Swires are survivors (in a much changed form) of that era of colonial expats. The Industrial Revolution forced manufacturing companies to identify new markets and cheaper production locations away from their home base. Manufacturers joined the traders in foreign locations and, whether making soap or automobiles, they still prosper today all over the world.

Financial services, global brands and consultancy have now joined the international arena and the expansion of internationals, transnationals and multinationals shows no sign of slowing down. A few years ago such organizations were synonymous with American industry but today they could just as easily be European, Japanese or Korean.

Despite constant localization of jobs, the sheer growth of international industry has resulted in a continual demand for expatriate workers – though whether this will continue is less clear. The underlying cause is that the local market needs their skills because it cannot supply these skills in the quantity required. The employer may be starting up an overseas concern or may need a watchdog to keep an eye on the tricky foreigners. Whatever the motivation, management is prepared to pay a premium for an expatriate member of staff; and when the authorization is given, the personnel department swings into action. Over the years the personnel departments of large companies have built up an expertise in the process of expatriation and are armed with overseas salary surveys, offshore pension proposals and cost of living charts.

This book is designed to help both existing and potential expatriates. Your motivation to work abroad is most likely that it is financially attractive to do so. Additionally, there are the prospects of career development, interesting foreign travel and a whole host of other personal aspirations. However, the field of overseas employment is a complicated one, with many traps and pitfalls. It has always seemed a little unfair to us, two personnel practitioners, that the first-time expatriate has very little idea of what to expect in terms of remuneration and benefits while working overseas. Equally, if you are working for a smaller company with little experience of sending people overseas, the company itself may not have much idea about how to structure an international assignment. The blind could be leading the blind.

This book is a guide, to be dipped into rather than read from cover to cover. It will help you with each stage of expatriation and equip you to deal with the jargon of the personnel manager responsible for the care of the company's expatriate staff. If it serves as a basis for negotiating your contract, so much the better – but never forget that a market exists for expatriates as with every other commodity, so don't price yourself out of it. Many personnel managers view the expatriate as an overpaid, overprivileged drone, whose job could be done twice as well by a local at half the cost. This is probably unfair but don't be surprised to encounter such attitudes, both within the home base company and at the overseas location.

One word of apology. We make no attempt to cover contract labour, the armies of non-skilled or semi-skilled workers who move around the Middle, and increasingly the Far, East. Our advice won't be of much help to the Mexican immigrant working on a Californian fruit farm. Such workers tend to be bound by collective labour contracts which are very different from the accepted concept of the 'expatriate'. For the moment, at least, the term applies overwhelmingly to the employee from the northern hemisphere or Australasia – probably a professional – working away from his home base. The contract will have a defined or implied time schedule, after which the expatriate is expected to move on or return to the home country. At the same time we have tried to avoid being too parochial: whatever the expatriate's country of origin, he or she will be faced with similar problems when leaving the home base.

Lastly, we make no attempt to catalogue local prices and conditions in the scores of countries that have large expatriate communities. This job is done well each year in *The Daily Telegraph Guide to Working*

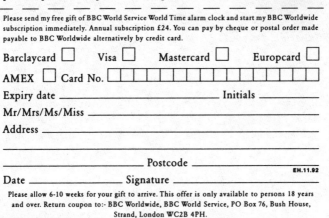

Abroad (published by Kogan Page). If one of our sections triggers off some detailed questions, there are plenty of information sources that may be pursued. We merely hope that the distilled experience of two 'old stagers' in the expatriate business will equip the new member of the fraternity with knowledge that would otherwise take many years to acquire through hard experience. Good luck with your assignment!

2. Assignment

Assignment is the employer's catch-all phrase for a period of employment which involves living and working in another country. If you are at the initial stage of simply thinking about working overseas, you should at least become familiar with some of the available options: not all overseas assignments are the same and they have different implications for the employee.

Expatriate assignments come in various shapes and sizes: there are still a few gin-sipping colonials seeing out their last days in the African sun; thousands of oil-rig hands work an endless cycle of four weeks in the Arabian desert followed by four weeks of domesticity in their home location; US-based technocrats are regularly sent to Hong Kong from their New York headquarters, for a three-year spell, to increase the Asian market penetration of the company's product line. An assignment might be for a one-year stretch in a jungle camp in Indonesia or an indefinite stay at a financier's hideaway on the beach in Bermuda. Despite the variety, you will find that the vast majority of arrangements fall into one of the following five classifications.

Out and back

This is a posting for a reasonably fixed period where an existing employee is sent from the home base to another location with the intention of returning when the assignment is over. Both the company and the individual presume that the transfer will lead to another more senior role on return and, while no guarantees are usually given, there is a commitment to repatriation.

In this situation, which probably constitutes the most common form of expatriation, conditions in the home base are often used as the reference point for the packaging of pay, benefits and other working conditions. They are also geared to the need for reintegration into the home country structure. There may be salary packaging difficulties for Third Country Nationals (TCN) – employees whose home base is not the company headquarters location. Nevertheless, the principle of keeping your base salary in line with your home country pay level is usually maintained.

Whether you come from the company's HQ or are a TCN, there is a chance that you will develop a taste for the expatriate life and, while assignment terms will reflect the intention of returning, most employers will be sufficiently flexible to recognize that you may need to stay longer or be transferred to another location. It is important to understand, from the outset, that there are very few absolutes in planning for expatriation; a healthy scepticism about the eventual conclusion of the assignment is essential.

The global railroad

Here the employee has no home base to speak of and accepts being sent to a number of different locations in succession, usually over a number of years. Each assignment is of indeterminate length, and a full career pattern may be a mixture of good and bad locations. A high degree of mobility is expected. The employee agrees to travel the world calling at various stations along the way, one of which may well be the country of origin.

The rewards for this nomadic and uncertain existence are often high. Pay is usually linked to a generous international standard and the unquestioning acceptance of difficult and frequently changing circumstances is cushioned by valuable allowances and a high quality lifestyle.

Often companies end up with an international staff cadre who have grown into the role of being full-time expatriates ready to move on to the next start-up or trouble spot. It is rare for anybody to be recruited, at the outset, for a full career span overseas except perhaps in the diplomatic service.

The mercenary

These are the 'soldiers of fortune' who hire themselves out to an organization for the purpose of completing a specific task, usually over an agreed period, and for a decent reward. A typical example would be a quantity surveyor contracted for a period of two years to play a part in the building of a new hospital in one of the Emirates. Here the terms of reference are extremely specific since there is no relationship either before or beyond the period of the assignment.

Terms and conditions for these types of assignment vary enormously. Like their military counterparts, individuals entering this field can expect rates of pay which can be defined by the dangers involved, the scarcity of specialist skills and, depending on the success of the mission, the promise of a substantial completion bonus. This is a field of expatriation which sets its own international rules and bears no resemblance to the more orthodox forms of assignment.

The rotator

Some may argue that this is not a form of expatriate assignment at all. The employee and family remain in the home base, with the bread winner travelling to the employment location on a prescribed schedule to perform work for several weeks, followed by an agreed period of leave in the home base. The cycle is repeated endlessly with no additional breaks. It could be for four weeks of work followed by four weeks of rest or any other workable rota which ensures that a particular task is performed by a combination of two or more employees sharing the workload.

This form of assignment is found most frequently in the oilfield sector where the manning of a rig is a 24-hour, seven days a week requirement. Oil rigs tend not to be located in major cities, so the concept of sending staff to operate them for short but arduous working periods is particularly appropriate.

A rotation assignment can be attractive for the employee since it allows for easy planning of longish periods with a family or for extended periods of travel during time off.

For the employer the cost of rotating is relatively cheap and the administration simple. Air fares are the most significant additional expense and accommodation is normally fairly basic since all that is required is a place for the employee to sleep when not working. Pay is usually the home base rate plus some premium for the inconvenience of being away from home for extended periods and, of course, there are no problems with reintegration.

Permanent

This speaks for itself. If an individual elects to go to another country to take up a job purely on local terms, the assignment can eventually end up being permanent. Conditions of employment are usually in line with local practice and, while some assistance may be given with relocation from the home base, there is little reference made at the outset to arrangements for going back. Here the distinction between a highly mobile expatriate, well rewarded for mobility, and the individual, willing to live in the country of his or her choice on whatever terms are available, is most marked.

A few lucky expatriates have managed to extract from their employers all the advantages of their mobile colleagues while, for all practical purposes, settling permanently in a foreign location. This usually happens when a normal three-year posting stretches out to ten or fifteen years. Maybe the individual has been forgotten by head office, or maybe they simply cannot find anyone to replace him. In any event, most expatriates will have come across some of these characters, firmly established in the local community and resistant to the idea of being transferred anywhere new.

In these situations most employers will respond by developing policies to integrate the assignee into the pay and benefits structure of the chosen country through a gradual withdrawal of expatriate conditions. Nobody should expect the rewards of mobility without accepting the disadvantages which are an inevitable by-product. However, you are always free to try!

The following chart summarizes the typical circumstances which create the need for each of the five categories of assignment:

Type of assignment	Circumstances of employment
Out and back	Employee requires development opportunity in another country
	No local staff available with the necessary skills for a given task
	Employee's skills will be in demand at some future date in the home base or elsewhere in the company
The global railroad	Large numbers of employees required in many countries
	Skills must be allocated at different times in many locations
	Resources to perform work are available from many countries
	Company has philosophy of a true international organization in that it believes in developing staff from all parts of the world rather than just from the country in which its HQ is located

	Returning the employee to a home base country is not an essential requirement
The rotator	Working conditions in the country of assignment are, typically, very harsh
	Work must be performed on a seven days a week basis, usually on single status
	Employees may be required in a number of different locations at different times depending on workloads and client requirements
The mercenary	A specific project requires skills which are not normally available to the employing company
	The project must be completed to specific deadline dates
	Once completed, the specialist skills will no longer be required by the employing company
Permanent	An individual requests an appointment in a specific country where he or she would like to remain indefinitely
	The employer has a vacancy and no local employee exists with the necessary skills
	The cost of relocating the employee would be no greater than the expense of recruiting and training an external local candidate to the same standard

✳   ✳   ✳

Assignment to the home base on expatriate terms?

Some companies manage to paint themselves into this corner. Take, for example, the case of a UK national working for a multinational computer manufacturer with headquarters in the US Mid-West. He joined the company in London and, after three years, transferred to world HQ in the US as an international employee. He confirmed his international credentials through a subsequent assignment to Switzerland before returning to the US. After five years overseas, and the proud owner of a Green Card, signifying his permanent resident status in America, he happily accepted full local terms in the US – now his adopted home. A year later, the company needed his services in the UK. By that time, of course, he had become a valuable asset and the company agreed to send him to the UK on the expatriate terms he demanded ... a house in the best part of Kensington, home leave air fares across the Atlantic each year, schooling costs paid etc.

* * *

You may not manage to achieve the ultimate deal of expatriate terms in your home country, but this story underlines the need to ensure that the nature of an assignment and its long-term consequences are clear.

3. The Good Expatriate?

Since there is a strong mutual desire on the part of the employer and you, the prospective assignee, to make the assignment successful, is it possible to define such a thing as an ideal expatriate profile? Behind this question lies an even more significant one: what can be done, once a candidate has been selected, to improve the chances of the expatriate assignment being totally successful? While the majority of postings work out reasonably well, in some 20–50 per cent of cases (according to various studies) the employee returns to the home base before the expected completion date and this is frequently because something has gone wrong; the family did not settle happily or the employee was not successful in his job. There are probably many other instances where the assignment ran its full course but the experience could have been happier or more productive if an individual with a different profile had been selected or a little more thought had been given to the pre-assignment preparation.

Selection for expatriation

The issue of selecting the right kind of applicant is, of course, largely dependent on where the chosen candidate has come from and where he or she is going to be sent. To this extent, there is probably no such animal as the ideal expatriate for every situation; one must think more in terms of certain types of profile being suited to particular environments and the avoidance of potential pitfalls. This, in turn, links the two factors of selection and preparation in that exposing the chosen candidate to the cross-cultural problems before the assignment begins will often make the difference between a reasonable level of adaptation and fulfilment and a highly successful entry, completion and exit.

Before looking at the specific cultural aspects, it is worth analysing the broader considerations when it comes to being considered for an appointment in another country. Becoming an expatriate is a screening process which, like any form of recruitment, whether internal or external, involves an initial matching of what the raw material has to offer and the skills and aptitudes required in the position.

Assuming you, the prospective candidate, can provide the academic and professional qualifications and skills needed for the job, you should be able to show evidence of some of the following if you are going to beat the probable 'competition':

- Experiences and exposure accumulated throughout your life which suggest that you will enjoy the challenge of adapting to an environment which is different from the one in which you currently live and work. This may be something obvious such as having worked abroad already or a natural facility in foreign languages. It may be the fact that you have parents of different nationalities or that you have travelled extensively overseas either on holiday or as a representative of an organization such as Voluntary Service Overseas or the Peace Corps. It could even be something less obvious such as social work performed in an ethnic minority community in your home country. Companies always look for this kind of exposure in their screening process and you should make an effort to highlight, in your application, anything which you think may give you an advantage.

- A clear explanation of your motives for wanting to live overseas. This will usually be investigated fairly thoroughly during interviews and you will be considered an average candidate if your only argument is that you are interested in people from other countries and want to experience their way of life. You should build your case carefully, concentrating on your overall career plans and specific aspects of life in the country to which you will move which interest you deeply. This may involve a considerable amount of preparation and research but your apparent familiarity with, and knowledge of, the place that you are planning to move to will put you head and shoulders above those who are unable to offer such carefully considered views. At all costs, you should avoid giving the impression that you want to move in order to escape problems in your home country. It is easy to make a number of disparaging comments about your home environment, or even the fact that you recently lost your driving licence, which will be seized upon as negative marks in the process of eliminating less suitable candidates.

- Your research into the country to which you hope to be expatriated should extend to a review of possible negatives which may be raised by the interviewer as to why somebody with your profile would not be able to adapt. There are some obvious issues. In Japan, for example, it is often difficult for local males to accept a female as their supervisor – especially when she is from a different culture. More subtle would be the difficulty encountered by a young single male moving to a predominantly Moslem country, like Malaysia, where there are few opportunities for social contact with the opposite sex. (This could be even more complicated if he had already worked overseas in, say, South America or parts of Africa where there is considerable opportunity to mix socially.) Your replies to questions on these sensitive issues will reveal a great deal about your suitability and you should be ready to respond constructively.

If you have a family, or you intend to move overseas with a partner, you must be able to demonstrate that they will have the necessary level of flexibility and tolerance to live for a number of years in an alien environment – possibly one which will have a far more profound effect on their day-to-day existence than it will on yours since you will at least have a reasonably familiar work routine to sustain you.

This advice may give the impression that, with a little careful thought, you can talk your way into an expatriate posting. Up to a point, this is true but it is crucial that, in building your arguments, you look honestly at whether you would actually be a good expatriate. All the points made in this section allow you to analyse the degree of risk that the assignment might well fail. If, in examining the evidence, you find that you are trying to deny the existence of problem areas, or have highly questionable motives for moving to a particular location, you should seriously consider terminating your application. At this relatively superficial level, you should be able to satisfy both your employer and yourself that you will be able to adapt successfully to expatriate life. It is worth knowing that there is a growing wave of interest in cross-cultural management problems and sensitivities among employers (evidenced by an increasingly large volume of published work on the subject). It will become more and more difficult to reach the shortlist of prospective candidates unless you are able to argue convincingly about your suitability.

Pre-assignment orientation courses

Assuming your credentials for 'good expatriate' status are accepted, your chances of becoming an even better one may be dramatically improved with a pre-assignment cultural orientation.

Packaged into a two- or three-day event, and usually conducted by a

HR CHALLENGES OF EXPATRIATION

In recent years many companies have had to respond to significant changes brought about by a downturn in previously expansionary economies and increasing pressure to internationalize their business activities abroad. For the company the establishment of operations is a major commitment often made to an environment which is unfamiliar. As experience develops the environment becomes less strange and the company more accustomed to local business practices which are generally different from those at home. For the employee the transfer overseas is more often than not a once in a lifetime experience which can be extremely demanding and challenging.

These changes have brought about new and unique challenges for Human Resource professionals in the way employees are managed and rewarded. The nature of the employment relationship with the transferred employee in particular is radically changed. It broadens to include many new areas such incentives, cost of living, housing, education, overseas taxation and social security. It also deepens into areas of concern which are normally considered to be private. This involvement in previously private related areas as well as the complexity of the additional knowledge base required makes the need for an effective framework of policies, practices and data sources essential.

Many larger and more internationally experienced companies have over a long period of time developed sophisticated international assignment policies. However, as an increasing number of smaller companies and indeed some larger ones, are entering the international scene for the first time it is important for them to quickly establish policies and practices particularly in the area of pay. The alternative is to establish expedient practices which become costly precedents in the longer-run.

The primary source of guidance for appropriate policy and practice is the business case for the transfer with the needs of the employee and his family coming a close second. The consequences of failure are two fold, the company risks significant financial loss, the employee and his family coming a close second. The consequences of failure are two fold, the company risks significant financial loss, the employee risks career and family life. It is therefore important to look at the whole transfer process and build in measures which will ensure that the needs of both the company and the employee are met which will lead to a better chance of success and reduce the likelihood of failure.

In order to develop an appropriate policy many companies put together a set of guiding principles. These principles establish company values and provide guidance which is generally timeless. However, they are often reinforced by practices which change in response to altering circumstances. These may be location specific, competitor influenced or more generally influenced by changes in local legislation or the social environment in the host location.

Other companies may use a detailed precedent-based approach. This approach often produces sets of detailed practices only very loosely bound in policies. This can lead to the evolution of an international assignment policy which is more like collective bargaining than focused on meeting the company's business needs.

When it comes to expatriate remuneration who are you short changing?

When you are negotiating expatriate remuneration packages, it's not just your employees' futures that are at stake. Decisions based on inaccurate data are bad for them, your company and you.

Which is why more international companies (1100 plus, at the last count) use ORC's expatriate remuneration database than anyone else's. They know that eliminating margin for error is an obsession for us. That's why we have more independent, impartial pricing agents collecting data, strategically located across Europe, Africa, the Middle East, Australasia, Central and South America and North America.

Of course, just having more agents isn't sufficient for us. We make sure they collect more data. Over 735 prices on 175 items, in fact from aspirin to apples, wine to washing machines, ORC's database provides the most comprehensive market basket picture you can buy. Because our pricing agents really are independent, our data suffers no distortion through inaccurate expatriate reporting.

Naturally, our thoroughness doesn't stop there.

In a rapidly changing world, we are anxious to ensure our clients obtain the latest remuneration information available. So, we up-date our home-host data more frequently than anyone else.

Some people think this is a little extreme but we wouldn't want you to compromise.

As you would expect, we cover all European Community, EFTA Central and Eastern European countries. After all, you don't want gaps in your knowledge, do you?

And because we recognise that no two companies operate in the same way we can customise our data to suit your precise needs.

We don't do all of this simply because we like crunching huge amounts of data. (Which, of course, we do!) We do it because this is the only way to deliver the defensive data that is so vital to your expatriate remuneration packages. Anything else would be second best, which isn't good enough for us, nor, we suspect, for you.

Having the world's best expatriate remuneration database is just one part of ORC's services for human resource and personnel professionals. For 60 years we have been helping world-wide organisations manage their human resources. If you would like more information about ORC's comprehensive range of products and services, including our expatriate remuneration database, call Siobhan Cummins on 071-222 9321. Then at least you won't take long to find out who you're short changing.

Organization Resources Counselors, Inc.

78, Buckingham Gate, London SW1E 6PE. Tel: 071-222 9321. Fax: 071-799 2018.

specialist organization, this preparatory training programme is normally aimed at both the employee and spouse. As well as providing practical information about a particular country, ranging from its political structure to the best places to shop, it serves an equally important function in preparing you for the cultural differences between the home base and the assignment location. In the UK, Employment Conditions Abroad Ltd and the Centre for International Briefing at Farnham Castle offer professionally run orientation programmes along these lines. Some companies, like the Swedish airline SAS, have established internal consultancies for this purpose which they are now offering as a service to other organizations.

Culture shock

An ability to recognize the cultural gulf between the way people in two countries behave and react, and come to terms with the differences, is one of the principal keys to successful expatriate life. Your reaction to an unknown and unpredictable environment may have a profound effect on how well you cope with your job, your family and the community in which you live. If you do not cope well, this is because the value systems

you normally employ to interpret what you see, hear and feel cease to function effectively in the new environment. This breakdown is commonly known as 'culture shock' which manifests itself, in its most extreme form, in often intolerable levels of debilitating stress. A pre-assignment training event can provide an important buffer to the potential effects of culture shock by familiarizing the expatriate couple with what may be uncertain and unpredictable in the new location. By exposing them to the culturally different standards which will apply to how they negotiate, discipline, praise, apologize, greet etc, it will accelerate the process of adjustment, both in a social and business context. (More advice and guidance on the effects of culture shock can be found in Chapter 25.)

The process of cultural adaptation may still become an endless uphill battle during your assignment despite your excellent credentials and thorough pre-assignment briefing. To this extent, whether you qualify as a good expatriate will remain difficult to predict.

Cultural distinctions can be put to a variety of uses during expatriation. A Dutchman, transferred to the United States, submitted a regular monthly expense report which included an item marked 'Friday flowers'. On being questioned about this unusual item, he claimed that, in Holland, it was the custom to take flowers home to one's wife each Friday evening to celebrate the arrival of the weekend. Since tulips were considerably more expensive in New York than in Amsterdam, he felt it only reasonable to claim the difference in cost.

*   *   *

4. Contracts

For the would-be first-time expatriate, obtaining your contract for Timbuktu or Billings, Montana is an exciting moment. In terms of signing on the dotted line and returning it to Head Office, it is probably the most dangerous moment of the assignment. Once signed, the contract will shape your job conditions for many years to come. Because of this, the contract should be treated with a great deal of respect.

There are ten specific areas that any decent expatriate contract should address.

Job, location and duration

These issues may sound obvious but may be important from a legal point of view at a later date. What exactly is the job title? Where is the main location of the job? Perhaps most important of all – what is the expected duration? Many contracts, just like their domestic counterparts, will be open ended, but it is a fact of life that jobs overseas tend to be a lot less stable than those at home. The other side of the coin is that no fast-rising executive wants to get stuck in a backwater for years and forgotten by Head Office. If this is an important factor for you, there should be a clause stating the expected length of the assignment and the intended method of repatriation, including some guarantees regarding a job on return.

Compensation and payment method

This is a critical area for the expatriate. In a domestic context the issue would be – how much? Overseas, how much is obviously still important, but there are other issues such as how the salary will be delivered. Will it all be paid in the local currency or will it be paid in the home currency or perhaps a third denomination? Will there be a mechanism to protect you against currency devaluations or exchange restrictions (see Chapter 9)? The nightmare of the expatriate accepting a highly paid two-year assignment only to find that 80 per cent of the salary is paid in non-convertible currency has occurred more than once.

Relocation

Relocation should cover any payments associated with moving expenses. A first-time expatriate might not appreciate the cost of moving and settling in at a foreign location. The company may, of course, offer to pick up the tab for everything, but usually you will be given a specific policy to follow. First on the list will be payment for shipping of household goods where an upper limit is often stated. Second, there will often be a furnishing allowance for the new house or perhaps a standard issue depending on your seniority and grade. Lastly, most companies will offer some sort of lump sum, maybe a month's salary, to cover miscellaneous expenses associated with the move. With these issues taken care of, the new expatriate only has to be concerned with initial travel expenses and the provision of temporary accommodation before moving into longer-term housing (see Chapter 5).

Housing

The type of housing provided is a central issue for an expatriate assignment. The ground rules for contractual purposes are the general nature of the housing, what proportion of the cost is paid by the expatriate, and who is responsible for the running costs and utilities. The formula for this may vary from the company paying for everything through an allowance to the cost being the responsibility of the expatriate. Suffice to say, the precise arrangement should be clearly stated in your contract to avoid difficulties at a later stage. (See Chapter 14.)

Allowances

Allowances are the jam on the expatriate bread and butter. Depending on the compensation package, a significant proportion of remuneration will come in the form of foreign service premiums, cost of living payments and compensation for hardship. Explanations regarding the finer points of allowances can be found in Chapters 7 and 11.

Car, club and schooling

After housing, the most substantial potential costs for any expatriate family are the running of a car, paying for the education of the children and organizing the membership of the local club. All these issues are dealt with in other chapters. In contractual terms, the expatriate should at least have an understanding in principle as to whether the company will pay for these or whether they are at the expense of the individual.

Vacation and vacation travel

Length of vacation for an expatriate is much the same sort of issue as it is for his domestic counterpart. However, many organizations, particularly in Europe, will offer more vacation to the expatriate on the basis that more recuperation is required. Equally, they may insist that you travel home to retain your cultural roots rather than spend time on safari or exploring steaming jungles. Apart from the amount of vacation, the contract letter should also spell out class of travel and whether a vacation air ticket can ever be taken as a cash benefit.

Tax

The whole issue of tax for the expatriate can be extremely complicated, involving such matters as tax equalization, responsibility for tax in the home country, local declaration policies etc. While all this can rarely be covered in detail in the contract letter, you should insist on having a statement on the overall tax policy. Failure to do this may have major financial implications if there is a subsequent dispute between you, your employer and the tax authorities.

Social security and insurance

This is perhaps the most intricate area of all, but again the overall principles should be addressed at the initial contract stage. The company will usually undertake to cover medical, life and accident insurance for you and your family, but the extent of the cover and the exclusion clauses should be checked carefully. The other major area of concern is the pension fund and whether it integrates, or fails to integrate, with arrangements in the home country. To a short-term expatriate, such arcane matters may be of little concern but as years overseas roll by, you may find yourself grossly disadvantaged because no agreement was made at the stage of signing the initial contract.

Separation

In the normal course of events separation will be at the end of your contract or as a result of a career move. You should, however, cover all contingencies. In the case of termination there should be some understanding that the company will pay for the transport of the family and household items back to the point of origin. This is indeed often a legal liability when the host country grants an employment visa and therefore will not usually pose a problem. There can, however, be some delicate discussions if the expatriate elects to work for a rival company and requires transport costs when it is clear he is returning to the same location in several weeks. In any event, planning for the worst contingency at the contract stage is much less complex than arguing about the matter if and when the employment relationship becomes less friendly.

If the above ten items are covered in the employment contract, both you and the company will at least have agreed on the essential aspects of your expatriate assignment.

International assignment manual

Most of the larger companies which employ a number of expatriates back up the individual assignment letter with a more detailed assignment manual. The letter, together the contents of the manual, will effectively make up the contract of employment. Given the complexity of expatriate assignments, no manual will ever manage to encompass every aspect of the assignment, although very experienced multinationals such as Shell and IBM have formulated policies on nearly every conceivable employment situation. A typical assignment manual will be split into the following areas:

Pre-assignment policies
- pre-assignment visit
- shipment and storage of household goods
- home country housing
- language courses

Relocation policies
- temporary living expenses
- travel expenses
- shipment of pets
- relocation allowances
- automobile purchase/sale

Assignment compensation policies
- base salary
- cost of living allowance

- housing allowance
- foreign service premium
- hardship allowance
- method of payment

General assignment policies
- education allowances
- benefit programmes
- holiday, home leave and vacation travel
- club membership
- emergency travel and evacuation
- repatriation policy

In many cases, there will be one detailed manual held by managers and the personnel department with a shorter, more user-friendly guide issued to the individual expatriate.

Legal complexities

The legal situation for international employment has always been a murky area as various jurisdictions are involved. Even the employer will often not always have a complete understanding of the legal structures in every country in which the company operates. As an expatriate employee, you are even less likely to understand the nuances of overseas employment law and therefore can be especially vulnerable.

* * *

Litigation seldom occurs in practice between an expatriate and his employer because it is rarely in the interests of either party. Imagine a typical employment situation. An American company recruits a Frenchman to work in Ghana. Which country's legal system would apply if there were a dispute between employer and employee? Would it be the USA's since it is an American company and the contract was perhaps signed at the US headquarters? Would it be France's since the employee is a French citizen? Or would it be Ghana's where the employee is working? The answer could be 'yes' to all three questions depending on the particular circumstances.

* * *

An international company will often give its employee a contract of employment which contains a clause such as 'this contract is agreed by both parties to be determined subject to the legal system of country X'. This may work but in practice you, the employee, or, by that time, ex-employee, may be able to take your case to the legal system of whatever country you see fit. The employer may refer to the original contractual clause and claim that the court has no jurisdiction, but for many tribunals this will cut no ice and the case will be heard anyway.

Some expatriate employment contracts state that the employee may be dismissed at any time without notice, irrespective of performance. This is presumably based on the assumption that the expatriate will neither have the inclination nor the legal expertise to challenge the decision in the local courts. While this may be true – you will nearly always take the money offered and head home – the legal basis for such an arrangement is weak. Most countries do not permit individuals to sign away their rights and will therefore consider the case regardless of what is stated in the contract.

*   *   *

An Englishman was recruited by a Panamanian company. He worked for four months training in the UK. He was then transferred to Norway, where he was put on the payroll of the Norwegian branch. Some 18 months later, he was dismissed for poor performance. He returned to the UK and took his case to an Industrial Tribunal claiming unfair dismissal. The tribunal found in his favour, and made the maximum award, even though he was not working for a UK company or in the UK.

*   *   *

For the vast majority of expatriates, the legal implications of the contract will never be tested and will therefore not be a significant issue. The important element will be to obtain a clear statement of the essential details of employment set down in the contract letter and in more detail in the assignment manual. Only in exceptional cases will you or the employer wish to become embroiled in local employment legislation. Even if you understand the language and can read the law books, you may find that it is one law for the locals and another for visitors. Equally, the company will try to avoid litigation, given that it will be bad publicity and could reveal certain practices that will attract the attention of the local authorities. The golden rules on expatriate contracts therefore seem to be: make sure they are written carefully at the start of the assignment, settle any differences internally and never become involved with the courts.

Secondment or local employment

Bearing in mind the points raised above on your legal status, it is important to have a clear understanding of who exactly is your employer during the assignment. If you continue under contract to the parent company, seconded to a location where no legal company status has been established, any claims you make will almost certainly be difficult to prove in the assignment country. Who will you threaten to take to court? On the other hand, if you are employed by the local legal entity (such as a subsidiary company of the parent organization), you will have a more concrete point of reference.

The differences between secondment and local employment may be important for other reasons:

- In Japan, if you are employed directly by a subsidiary operation, you will automatically be covered by local labour legislation. This means that participation in the locally established company pension plan and Japanese state social security schemes will be mandatory (not necessarily to your advantage because of the restrictions on exporting assets from Japanese plans if you subsequently return to your home-based employer). If you are seconded as an employee of a company outside Japan, you will be excluded from the state schemes and membership in a non-Japanese company pension scheme will be permitted.
- French employees 'detached' from their home-based employers are less likely to be able to continue their participation in French social security programmes than those who remain 'attached'.
- Severance benefit entitlements in the home base country are much more likely to be enforced if a secondment arrangement is established. The disadvantage here, of course, is that tax liabilities in the home country on severance payments are much more difficult to avoid.

You would be well advised to investigate the consequences of either form of employment status before accepting an appointment. The probability of a problem arising is fairly remote but, as always, a healthy curiosity about what lies ahead, and a little gentle prodding in the early stages of discussion, may help to avoid disillusionment and a frustrating sense of being ill-informed if problems should subsequently occur.

5. Journey's Start

The contract has been negotiated, you have signed on the dotted line and you have gone home and delivered the bombshell to the family. At this stage the hard work really begins. The guiding principle should undoubtedly be 'the more you sweat in training, the less you bleed in war'. Put another way, groundwork at the beginning of the expatriate assignment saves time and heartache later on.

Guides and briefing groups

Depending on your circumstances much of this may be provided by the company – if not, it will be up to you to dig around the local library. The most up-market approach is that of the residential briefing group designed for the whole family. This approach, as detailed in Chapter 3 lays on a two- or three-day briefing where experts deliver information on every aspect of the assignment and the new country. You will hear about the climate, the state of the economy, local customs and business practices, the food etc. Of course, such a seminar is only as good as the experts you get. The danger is that this sort of processed information may be somewhat out of date if delivered by an old buffer who worked in the country 20 years ago. Mostly, however, such briefing groups offer excellent value for money and the first-time expat should try to persuade his company to finance a visit to such a seminar. Failing a briefing group, there are usually plenty of guides to a new country, whether in the form of travellers' tales, a geography textbook or a Lonely Planet travel guide. Many companies prepare their own country guides, designed specifically for the expatriate, providing details of climate, clothing requirements, visa and medical formalities and the electrical system. A period of carefully focused study will certainly lessen the culture shock after arrival.

Pre-assignment visit

In the days of ships, trains and five-year assignments before the first leave, the concept of a pre-assignment visit was unusual. The age of cheap jet travel has changed this viewpoint and many companies will approve of, and often insist on, a pre-assignment visit. This may be for the employee alone or more usually for the employee and spouse, rarely with the children in tow. The idea of the visit will be to get a flavour of the overseas location, meet some colleagues and start looking around for suitable housing. The risk is, of course, that the first impression will be so bad that the assignment is refused, but that is better than staying a month and then deciding to leave. You should expect that any pre-assignment visit will only be for a few days and the company may well insist on economy travel.

Housing in the home base

One of the main worries for the expatriate, assuming he is a house-owner, is what to do with the home he is leaving. In times of booming property markets, it may be attractive to sell up and bank the proceeds. Generally, however, this is an unwise strategy when first taking an overseas assignment. For some reason, the contract may not work out and you will need a home base again sooner than expected. You may time your period overseas just as the property market takes off, making the house you sold out of your financial reach in just a few years. Later on, of course, if a string of overseas assignments is likely, the calculation becomes a little different. The long-term expatriate and his family may no longer feel the need for a home base. They may decide to invest in property elsewhere or simply move out of the property market altogether. This sort of decision should only be made after a few years' experience of working overseas.

If you are not going to sell, the decision on the house comes down to letting it out or keeping the place empty for family use during vacations and home visits. Letting is usually the obvious choice for financial, and often tax, reasons. An empty house available for the expatriate in his home country will often affect his non-resident status and thereby jeopardize his tax situation. Advice on letting is simple. First, never go for a 'do-it-yourself' arrangement; always appoint a good agent and prepare a legal contract. Second, persuade the company to pay for the letting and administration fees.

Even the most meticulous arrangements with the house will not guarantee good tenants or a trouble-free lease, but at least they will improve your chances. There are few things more frustrating than seeing home leasing arrangements fall apart when you are thousands of miles away and powerless to do anything about it. As a general rule of thumb, assume that any good agent will take between 10 and 15 per cent of your rental income each month and at best your rental return will be in the region of 5–8 per cent of the capital tied up in the house.

Storage of goods

Unless you take everything with you (an option few companies allow), or friends and relatives can be persuaded to help, you will have to arrange for commercial storage of your possessions while you are away. Most towns offer some sort of warehouse arrangements but you pay for what you get. A secure, dry, well-insured storage facility is expensive. Happily, most companies will pick up the cost of this service, at least for the usual list of family possessions. There are many specialist storage services available – for the much loved classic car or for the fine wine collection – but you may find that the personnel department will baulk at underwriting these types of cost. Unlike housing, when it comes to the car, unless it is a family heirloom, selling is invariably the way to go. If you are lucky, you may work for an employer who makes a cash allowance to compensate for the additional depreciation you will undoubtedly suffer from a forced early sale.

Shipment of goods

Companies vary on their policies regarding shipment of goods. At one extreme, they may insist on mobility and travelling light. This means a fully furnished apartment at the location and a small shipping allowance. Other companies are much more generous with the shipping allowance and allow furniture to be shipped. Few companies will accept the shipment of utility items – stoves, fridges, TVs etc – because of the cost of transport and the problems of incompatibility with the electrical system at the location.

What to take must always depend on the sort of location you are heading for and your domestic circumstances. An assignment in most places in Europe, America or the Far East will mean that most items of domestic goods will be available locally. A spell in one of the more obscure African countries may necessitate you taking everything you are allowed to ship. A bachelor may not feel the need for much apart from a bed, table, chair and stereo system, whereas a family may want to reproduce their home location environment almost in its entirety. However big or small the shipment, make sure that it is insured door to door, that you have a complete inventory and that the documentation is correct. Even if you use the most reputable shipper and take every precaution, don't be surprised if you add to the list of expatriate horror stories. These range from minor breakages, through petty pilfering to months stuck in Customs, even total disappearance. Therefore, the cautious expatriate never ships the family silver or the precious antiques. Even a mundane insurance claim will take months to sort out and the assessor will rarely allow the value that you yourself put on your goods and chattels.

One last aspect of shipping concerns the family pet or pets. The seasoned expatriate knows that transporting the family mutt is more time-consuming, more expensive and far more emotive than moving the rest of the family. (This subject is discussed more fully in Chapter 16.)

Medical and documentation

Ensuring that you and your family are fit for the journey is a necessity. So too is obtaining all the necessary immunizations, malaria pills etc. These aspects are fully covered in Chapter 18.

✳ ✳ ✳

A businessman arrived in Lagos, Nigeria many years ago having had a yellow fever shot five days before rather than the required six. The concerned immigration official offered him two choices – get back on the next plane or have a 'booster shot' in an airport clinic that looked like a badly kept butcher's shop. Fortunately, some minutes of discussion uncovered a third option which involved a large transaction of cash.

✳ ✳ ✳

All sorts of other documentation may be required for your stay overseas. Birth certificates, marriage certificate and educational qualifications come to mind. Local officials can be touchy about issuing work permits if the expatriate does not have the correct documentation. At least one company has been known to fake engineering degree certificates to ensure that its expatriates pass the highly artificial education require-ments that apply to expatriate workers. Also, if young children are to travel on their own, make sure that they have their own passports before departure.

With all this done, the tickets, passports and cash in hand, the expatriate and his family can head for the airport secure in the knowledge that they have at least done as much groundwork and preparation as possible.

Pre-assignment checklist

- Home country briefing
- Language tuition
- Reading list
- Renewal of passports
- Entry requirements – visas, qualifications etc
- Return of company car
- Flight arrangements
- Return of contract acceptance letter
- Medical examinations
- Immunisations up to date
- Dental check
- Door-to-door estimates of shipment
- Obtain inventory of goods
- Check transit time for carrier
- Ensure insurance of personal effects
- Obtain estimates of home storage
- Arrange insurance of stored goods
- Transfer effects into store
- Inform gas, telephone and electricity
- Arrange letting of home property/power of attorney
- Sale of private car
- Clear personal tax and finances
- Arrange education for children either at home or at assignment location
- Cancel magazine subscriptions
- Arrange for forwarding of mail
- Pack travel bags
- Cash for first few days
- Contact points at location

If you have managed all that, breathe a sigh of relief and head for the airport!

Temporary accommodation

A new expatriate may often forget that a shipment of goods can take several months to arrive. Unless the family has been sleeping on the floor for several weeks before departure or fully furnished quarters are being arranged from day one in the new location, some sort of temporary accommodation is required. This usually means the local hotel at company expense. Any family who has survived a few weeks of this knows that such stays are best kept to a minimum – a hotel room can be terribly depressing after a few days. The company will usually provide some sort of disturbance allowance in the first month to help with all the small purchases required when moving in. A concerted effort to organize accommodation early on is one of the best ways of minimizing the effects of culture shock and home sickness. Get to work!

Arrival checklist

This is not as long as the departure checklist but the main items to work on are:

- Local housing (discussed in Chapter 14)
- Bank account and driving licence – get them as soon as possible
- Work permit, registration, dependent passes – use the local company 'Mr Fixit' to help you
- Schooling for children (discussed in Chapter 17)
- Car (discussed in Chapter 19)
- Domestic help (see Chapter 21)

Mao Tse Dong said that 'every journey starts with the first step' and he could have been talking about expatriate assignments instead of revolutions. At the beginning there always seems so much to do, and all the work comes when anxiety and insecurity are probably at their highest level. How the expatriate and his family prepare for the assignment may well determine the success or failure of the following years.

6. Salary

Pay, salary, remuneration ... whatever word is used, it remains the primary concern for most expatriates. You may well venture overseas because you like jungles or deserts, because you have always wanted to learn Swahili or simply because you feel the need for a change. However, what keeps you away from 'kith and kin' usually involves attractive rewards and the surplus cash that can be amassed.

The problem for an expatriate is that the reward criterion is rarely as clear as it would be for his home-based colleague. There is no clear 'market rate' for the expatriate as staff are usually recruited at the home base and then dispatched to the assignment location. On arrival you can, of course, compare yourself with other expatriates of different nationalities and from different countries. This comparison is difficult, however, and often misleading. First, a Portuguese expatriate may not justify the same rate for the job as a Swiss expatriate, given their different home-based remuneration. Most expatriate packages are driven by the base salary and so many of the cost of living allowances and benefits will also vary widely depending on point of origin. Second, there is always the tendency to make a partial comparison rather than compare each package as a whole. This is the cherry-picking approach of finding that your next-door neighbour (say, a German expatriate) in the Congo has a higher hardship allowance but conveniently forgetting that he pays a housing deduction while you do not. To get a true picture all the elements of the expatriate package must be costed and compared before any judgement can be made.

The complexity of comparison is one reason why there are so few expatriate salary surveys available to give potential expats an idea of the 'going rate' for the job. Moreover, the truth is that when everything has been costed out all expatriate assignments are extremely expensive ventures for the company.

A typical breakdown of costs would be:

	% of total
Base salary	30
Bonus	5
Cost of living	14
Pension	5
Insurance	1
Housing	16
Cost of tax and social security payments	6
Medical costs	3
Vacation and travel	8
Transfer costs	8
Miscellaneous (car, school fees etc)	4
Total	**100**

Even with a fairly typical base salary (say £40,000 pa) applied to the above breakdown, the company will be faced with a total bill in the region of £125,000 for a year of expatriate service. This, needless to say, excludes any costs of actually doing business. The cost-conscious employer will therefore do his sums carefully before committing to an additional expat and will expect his pound of flesh. The days when expatriate assignments were cushy numbers have long gone for most international companies.

The expatriate, for his part, has to study all the components of the company offer to work out precisely the net benefits. How you approach this exercise depends on the particular structure of the salary package. It is also affected by allowances given, tax treatment and currency issues. The next seven chapters address these issues. Only when the expatriate fully understands all the implications of the employment offer will a clear understanding of the net benefits be possible. In other words, do not crack open the champagne before doing your sums and knowing that you can afford the price of the bottle!

7. The Balance Sheet

There are many variations on the theme of how the net value of an expatriate's salary is calculated – some rough and ready, others sophisticated mathematical formulae. The nearest thing to a standard approach is the 'balance sheet' used in various forms by many international companies. The roots of the balance sheet approach can be found in post-war American personnel departments. At that time American companies were experiencing a rapid increase in the numbers of expatriates being sent to different parts of the world. What was required was a system with some kind of internal logic which could be explained to employees and which was based on independent reference data in order to arrive at the final calculation. Of all the expatriate payment systems the balance sheet approach does manage to achieve these two aspects, although it has some inherent disadvantages, not least being the complexity of the full-blooded balance sheet approach.

The term 'balance sheet' is somewhat misleading as it implies an accountancy approach which rarely exists in practice. The overall philosophy is to cost out the expenses of living overseas and balance, or maybe neutralize is a better word, the expenses against those that would have been incurred in the home country. A phrase that employers often use is 'no worse off'. This means that a basic home country reference salary can be retained throughout the assignment and any incentive payments related to the overseas posting can be clearly identified. The balance sheet is a dynamic approach as it takes into account changes in cost of living, tax rates etc. and requires review on a regular basis.

Looked at all at once, particularly when presented by a consultant, the balance sheet can appear somewhat daunting. To make sense of it the best approach is to break it up into its constituent parts, which are:

- Home-based salary reference
- Discretionary spending portion
- Cost of living
- Housing

- Tax equalization
- Overseas incentives (see Chapter 11)
- Insurance and social security arrangements (see Chapter 23).

Home-based salary reference

A common pitfall of the expatriate package is that it is not broken into constituent parts. This does not matter much in the foreign location but can cause serious problems subsequently when returning to a job in the home country. Without a base reference salary the employer may find it difficult to fit the expatriate back into any domestic salary structure, and you may feel cheated by a base which seems small in comparison to the benefits overseas. The balance sheet approach avoids this problem by starting with a clearly defined base reference salary which fits into the home salary structure, often using the company job evaluation plan. This base salary is retained throughout the assignment and annual reviews are undertaken using the same policy guidelines as the domestic location. A problem may, of course, arise regarding co-ordination between the overseas manager and the home base which needs to be solved by careful communication.

A basic part of the logic of the balance sheet is that the reference salary for an employee from one country will be different from that of another doing exactly the same job. The Swiss engineer will be on Swiss rates, the Indian engineer on Indian rates. Some companies find this approach unacceptable and come up with a modified version that builds in minimum base salaries for the job or allocate expatriates into a simplified group of 'nationalities' which prevent large discrepancies in base salaries. Although this dilutes the logic of the exercise, it can avoid problems among the expatriates and with locals in high salary markets.

The base salary is generally used as a reference for purposes of insurance and pension arrangements regardless of other allowances paid as a result of the assignment location.

Spendable income

Following the logic of neutralizing cost differences as a result of an overseas posting, the next step is to identify the proportion of spendable income in an expatriate's salary. To do this, home country spending patterns must be reviewed based on level of income and family size. This is where government or consultancy statistics must be used to track a spendable income curve. The exercise may sound complex but the underlying logic is simple: to estimate what portion of the home salary remains after the deduction of monthly living expenses. Again, this portion will differ between nationalities – with perhaps the German retaining a much higher proportion of discretionary income than the American.

Many expatriates find this approach a little cold-blooded as there is no such thing as an 'average' or 'typical' expenditure pattern. One family may spend all their money at casinos, the next may live on bread and water and invest everything they save, but for the purposes of the balance sheet overall assumptions have to be made.

Cost of living allowance

Having arrived at a percentage figure of spendable income, a comparison can be made between the cost of living at home and at the place of assignment. If costs are higher, a cost of living allowance (COLA) may be paid to compensate. Cost differences are examined in relation to the spendable portion of the salary, not the whole salary. Again, a number of assumptions must be made regarding the expenditure pattern of the expatriate family – what constitutes the 'basket of goods' used to make the cost comparisons. First, items are extracted that are covered in other parts of the compensation package. If, as is normal in an assignment, housing is provided to the expatriate, it must be excluded from the basket of goods. Likewise, a company car with running expenses paid will not figure in cost comparisons. What is left are the everyday items of life ranging from the goods on a supermarket shelf to the cost of entertainment and the price of drinks and cigarettes at the local bar. Again, the services of government or consultant statistics are necessary to build up a shopping basket survey of prices in all the locations involved. This may be just New York compared with, say, Paris – a relatively simple exercise, but a large multinational using this approach will need tables for perhaps a dozen nationalities against 20 or 30 expatriate locations. Such a project results in a formidable statistical exercise, and is only practical if undertaken by a consultancy, with the results shared among a number of companies. Cost of living analyses are usually expressed in the form of an index where the home country costs are represented by a base 100 and the expatriate location by the relevant relational figure. For example, a spendable income of £10,000 in the home base (100) would generate a COLA of £12,000 in a location where the equivalent cost of living index figure is given as 120.

The nuances of the COLA could fill a book on their own, and is a favourite topic for any expatriate. The assumptions regarding the basket of goods may be queried. Often consultancies come up with two tables – higher costs for the new expatriate and a lower set of figures for the longer-term employee who has learnt cost-effective shopping in the location. COLAs are based on the difference between costs in two locations and so this gives rise to disputes regarding the different rates of inflation in the two places. What seems a high increase in cost to the expatriate may in fact be less than the increase taking place in his home country – something easily overlooked when living abroad. The statistical base is often queried by expatriates, particularly if the tables are not reviewed frequently. Organizations compiling the tables will often use an army of local staff to check current prices in the locations in an effort to keep their information up to date.

In the last analysis, the COLA can only be an approximation of the cost differential between the home base and the assignment location. There are too many variables and quirks of human nature to give the exercise any real scientific credibility. Many families actually view the allowance as additional income rather than an equalizing mechanism. Is the US$7000 monthly allowance in Tokyo really spent on price differentials? Does the family in Lagos really buy on the open market or is there a pipeline of unofficial imported foods? Certainly, the single employee and the high salary earner will tend to see the COLA as a straight benefit whereas the larger family unit, faced with weekly food bills, will view the allowance in a more realistic light.

Accurate or not, the concept of a COLA fits in with the logic of a balance sheet and therefore is an essential constituent part of the overall equation.

Housing

Housing is dealt with in some detail in Chapter 14. For the expatriate, housing and housing costs will always be a major issue and as such occupy an important part of the balance sheet. Normally, housing is excluded from the cost of living element, being a major issue in its own right. The actual treatment of housing costs depends on the degree of detail required by the company. A common broad-brush approach is to assume that housing at home costs a certain fixed percentage of salary and make the appropriate deduction from the package. Assignment housing is then provided by the company. A more painstaking approach is to work out costings by country of origin and by income/family size. The end result according to the company is that the employee should be 'no better and no worse off' as a result of the overseas assignment.

The flaw in this approach concerns the housing situation of the expatriate in his home country. If the family is renting at home, the cessation of rental costs will produce a new income stream. If, on the other hand, the home property is owned there are major financial implications: keeping a house empty will incur financial penalties; renting will provide an income. Logically, this should be taken into account in the balance sheet, although few companies will go into this level of detail.

Tax equalization

The tax implications (in both home and host country) are a subject in themselves and are covered in Chapter 12. For the purpose of the balance sheet, tax may be factored into the equation so that the tax take on base salary is approximately the same as it would have been in the home country. Any actual tax arising on the package in excess of this amount is borne by the employer. Again, the detailed approach involves the offices of an accountant and a number of detailed calculations. A simpler but more approximate solution can be to levy a percentage figure that roughly equates to the home tax take. The company is then responsible for any additional tax levied on the individual in the host country.

Before the balance sheet is completed, there are some other loose ends to be tied up. Social security payments, related back to the home country, will usually be deducted from the base salary. Any additional premiums for undertaking the assignment, ie foreign service premium and hardship allowance etc, are factored in net of tax. The final calculation provides a grand total which is the overseas net salary:

HOME BASE SALARY

plus

FOREIGN SERVICE PREMIUM AND HARDSHIP ALLOWANCE

plus

COLA

minus

HOUSING DEDUCTION

minus

HOME COUNTRY TAX

gives

OVERSEAS NET SALARY

In this discussion nothing has been mentioned about currency, a significant omission as fluctuating exchange rates can wreak havoc on the logic of the balance sheet. For those who wish to study the implications of currency, turn immediately to Chapter 9 for an examination of this issue.

The virtues of the balance sheet approach are also its failings. The method divides the constituent parts of the expatriate package into separate compartments. Each problem is then approached systematically and costs are measured. The jigsaw is then assembled to generate a final net figure. Its strengths therefore are logic, consistency and an ability to explain each calculation. Its weakness is the monster that can easily be created when the logic is taken to extremes. Each part of the package can become a nightmare of complex calculations, with frequent adjustments for inflation, currency changes and change in status of the expatriate. The administrator has to employ an army of clerks and consultants to keep all the figures up to date, only to find that the expatriate employees do not accept or understand the logic of the exercise in the first place. Such a scenario is bad when looking at several nationalities in a handful of locations. It may become quite unmanageable when dealing with scores of nationalities all over the world.

Because of the inherent complexities of the balance sheet many companies have moved to a modified approach that introduces standard salaries and only one cost of living base, against which all other locations are measured. Other companies have abandoned the approach altogether in an attempt to find something simpler. Many of the more traditional 'colonial' organizations never adopted the balance sheet in the first place, preferring to emphasize the required standard of living in the assignment country rather than comparisons with the home country. Nevertheless, the balance sheet remains one of the most logical approaches to quantifying expatriate packages and, even if not fully applied, has influenced, in one form or another, most of the major expatriate employers; it will continue for many years to come.

Balance sheet example

The typical figures and conceptual model on page 49 help to illustrate the way in which the balance sheet approach, in its simplest form, actually works.

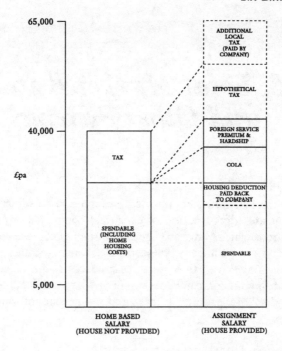

	Homebase	Overseas
		£
Home base gross salary		40,000
Less tax	(12,000)	(12,000)
		(hypothetical)
Less housing deduction at 10%	–	(4,000)
Plus COLA from tables		8,000
Plus Foreign Service Premium at 15%		6,000
Equals net	28,000	38,000

This example assumes that there are no other deductions from the home base for saving plans, pension contributions etc. The COLA will normally be adjusted on a quarterly basis, taking into account currency fluctuations and inflation in the home and host locations. The COLA tables are provided for various family sizes and expenditure patterns, and are calculated on a proportion of the total salary representing the spendable element. Tax and social security deductions may be on a hypothetical basis (estimated). With the US, where an actual tax return must be made for the expatriate, a complex balancing mechanism is required to proportion out the individual and company tax obligations.

8. Local Market Rates and Other Systems

Although the balance sheet approach has come to be something of a standard in the administration of expatriate compensation, there are other methods which better suit the circumstances of some assignment locations and some company philosophies. Many of the approaches are hybrid, adopting a variety of features tailored to the nature of the assignment. If your company does not use a balance sheet method, it is probable that the package is prepared using one of three other approaches.

Host country (local) salary package

The local rate approach is essentially the opposite starting point from the balance sheet. Whereas the balance sheet starts with the expatriate's home country base salary and retains this base throughout subsequent calculations, the local rate approach fits the expatriate into the compensation system of the local market. This may come together with modifications which offer housing assistance or other premiums, but the starting point is the going rate for the job in the country to which the expatriate is posted. Naturally, this raises a few fundamental problems which restrict the use of the host country approach. Clearly, if the market rates in the country of assignment are lower, the proposed package will only be interesting to expatriates coming from equally low paid home markets. On the other hand, an expatriate from a high paying base country will not find any expatriate location, using this approach, where the compensation package will be attractive.

Despite its shortcomings, there are situations where the host country approach can prove useful. First, the net comparison will usually be made taking into account the local tax situation which, if favourable, will add to the attractions of a locally based compensation package. Hong Kong is a prime example of this where total tax rates do not go above 15 per cent, making the net value of the local salary package attractive, compared with many European countries. Where this is the case and in situations where market rates are attractive, the company looking for a simple solution may decide to offer expatriates the local rates. Most of the package would then follow local conditions concerning tax, insurance and social security, but may be modified to offer some sort of housing allowance or expatriate premium. The two advantages of this approach are simplicity and compatibility with the local employees. The disadvantage is that no real underlying logic is applied to the expatriate deal, so that when it comes to a transfer to another country, there are no arrangements for the transition. Moreover, a company with expatriates in many countries is unlikely to be able to use the local approach everywhere and will thus be saddled with inconsistencies regarding the treatment of its expatriate workforce. Additionally, the absence of any reference point to the home country will often make re-entry difficult to handle.

It is often the Third Country National (TCN) who can be placed on the local market rate because the company will not feel the same pressure to integrate a TCN into the overall expatriate structure. This may not be a bad outcome for the expatriate, depending on the details of the package. A good base and bonus with some provision for housing, education of children and perhaps an annual vacation ticket will cover most requirements. Moreover, the 'full' expatriate may find his net deal less attractive taking into account deductions for tax equalization, housing and social security.

If you find yourself on this type of package be aware of the advantages and disadvantages. The approach is simple and straightforward, without any need to worry about complex cost of living calculations. Equally, the annual review will be based on local market conditions, not some theoretical reference salary back in the home country. You pay your own tax and may be expected to join the local medical and pension arrangements. You are not seen as 'different' by the local managers except that you may have a housing allowance. So far so good. The down side is that a host country package may not insulate you against local inflation or violent currency swings. The logic of re-entry to your home country is not good, as you have no reference salary with additions for hardship and cost of living. This may not matter if you are returning to a new company but can complicate arrangements if it is an internal transfer.

International reference

Some big companies use this approach for all their expatriates and it has many advantages. For the employer the big disadvantage is that it is usually expensive because it treats the whole expatriate workforce as one group for pay and conditions. Thus it has to pitch rates high enough to be attractive for the expatriate from a wealthy country and by doing so gives the expat from a poorer country an over-generous deal (and eventually a problem in trying to re-adjust to the low wage levels in the home country).

The make-up of the package is simple. All expatriates are required to sign an international contract which pays base salaries determined by the 'international market' – perhaps the oil industry or international aircrew. There may be an element of currency protection by making up the base in a basket of currencies including the dollar and the ECU (European Currency Unit). All assignment locations have a supplementary payment in the form of a co-efficient to measure hardship and local levels of cost. Europe and America might start off with a 1.15 co-efficient of base rising to 1.7 of base for locations such as Angola or Nigeria. Everyone has a standard deduction for tax and possibly housing wherever they are located. Lastly, expatriates usually belong to a global, offshore insurance and retirement fund which operates outside any of the national administrations.

The great advantage of this type of approach is that it is easily understood and treats all expatriates on an equal basis. It is very effective if mobility in company is held at a premium and many executives spend most of their careers overseas. You will usually only encounter the international approach when joining one of the big international companies, particularly in the oil industry.

Budget method

This type of package is a little different from either the balance sheet, local or international method. It stems mainly from a foreign tradition where administrators were sent out on long periods of secondment. Essentially, this approach assumes a home-based salary which may not be very high but will be enough to meet domestic expenses and achieve a savings element. On top of this an allowance in the currency of the location is given to maintain a lifestyle appropriate to the level of the job in that location. This is where the budget method differs from the balance sheet, as the local allowance level is based entirely on lifestyle required in the local community. Thus a low paid administrator might enjoy a high local allowance in order to maintain the correct image in the overseas location. Clearly, this has applications in diplomatic and civil service posts but is also seen as a reasonable approach in some of the more traditional companies operating in developing countries.

The advantage of such an approach is that it may provide you with a splendid house and lifestyle while in the location. The disadvantage is the shock of returning to the home country and adjusting to the old, less glamorous lifestyle.

There are, of course, many variations on the theme and you need to study your contract and conditions of service to identify which particular approach is being adopted by your company. They all have advantages and drawbacks, so it is not a question of finding the perfect system – which simply does not exist. However, you need to know where you stand in the company that either does not have any logical approach or mixes the various methods up. This is particularly dangerous as the result will nearly always be to your disadvantage. Surprisingly, many fair-sized companies and their personnel departments are still very amateurish when it comes to handling their expatriates. Because of this you may be able to argue for some changes of approach which will be conceded on the strengh of the logic used.

Local rate salary

Expatriate A goes to Hong Kong and is offered a package denominated wholly in local currency. The HK dollar is pegged to the US dollar at the rate of 7.8 to 1. No cost of living or overseas allowances are provided, but a housing allowance is given to assist with the high cost of rents. The expatriate is enrolled on the local insurance, medical and provident fund schemes.

Base salary: HK$702,000 @ 7.8 = US$90,000
Local tax @ 16.5% HK$(115,830)
Housing allowance: HK$30,000 a month (all spent on housing)
Net salary: HK$586,170 @ 7.8 = US$75,150

Note: although the maximum tax rate in Hong Kong is currently 15 per cent, housing provision is also taxed on a nominal sum equivalent to 10 per cent of salary. Hence the overall tax rate of 16.5 per cent.

International salary

Expatriate B joins an international company which uses US dollars as its base payment system. The contract provides fully furnished housing in Hong Kong and the company pays any local tax obligation. The contract provides for a non-contributory offshore pension and insurance plan.

Payment is made offshore in US dollars. The base salary is again US$90,000 per annum.

Base salary:	US$90,000
Overseas co-efficient for HK @ 1.3:	US$27,000
Tax pool at 15%:	US$(13,500)
Housing deduction at 10%:	US$(9,000)
Net salary:	US$94,500

Budget method

Expatriate C works for the government and has a home country salary equivalent to US$50,000. This continues to be paid into his home country bank account and he is responsible for tax and social security payments on this amount. He is posted to India where he is paid a local allowance equivalent to US$40,000, at present 1.35 million Indian rupees. Housing and local tax are payable from the local allowance.

Base salary:	US$50,000
Tax at, say, 20%:	US$(10,000)
Local allowance:	US$40,000
(exchange controls prevent any of this allowance being repatriated to the home country)	
Net salary:	US$80,000

9. Currency

For simplicity we have omitted currency considerations in the explanations of the various approaches to expatriate compensation. In reality, the expatriate has to be careful about currency fluctuations to prevent an attractive package turning into a disaster. Using the yen as an example, a Japanese executive, who was unfortunate enough to have accepted his expatriate salary denominated entirely in US dollars over the last ten years, would have lost 20 per cent of the value of his salary in domestic terms. Of course, this sort of equation works both ways; for example, a British expat paid in Singapore dollars over the same period would have increased his remuneration, in home terms, by 30 per cent, purely on currency appreciation. This is particularly important when one considers that most expatriates usually have some home country expense commitments and will eventually want to repatriate their savings.

In practice, most expatriate deals include some element of salary protection so that the employee (and, to some extent, the employer) is cushioned against wild swings in currency or hyperinflation in the assignment location.

Split salaries

A simple form of currency protection is to split the salary of the expatriate and deliver one portion in the local currency and the other in the home country currency. This is not always easy as in some countries the company is subject to local legislation which demands that all salaries are paid in local currency. In such situations it will be difficult for the tax authorities to enforce such a ruling without having access to bank accounts in the home country. As long as a 'reasonable' amount is delivered to the expat in local currency the company may choose to make other payment arrangements in the home country.

Where there are no exchange restrictions the salary can be paid entirely in the home or host country. Some companies offer the expatriate the choice regarding what proportion should be paid where.

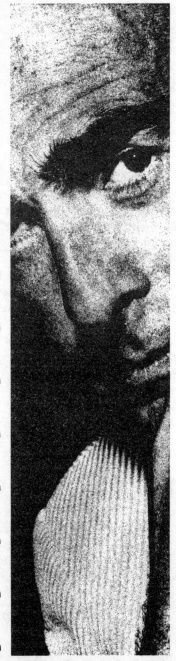

If you're working abroad, or about to return home, you need go no further than the nearest telephone and call Barclays Expatriate Advisory Service. Whether your needs are simple or complex, we can give specialist advice on the most tax efficient investment of income or capital. We also have a range of deposit accounts paying interest gross on sterling or foreign currency. Or if you haven't yet taken up your overseas posting you might find one of our Country Reports useful. They are available for thirty different countries and contain information covering everything from economic conditions to local customs and etiquette.

I'M WORKING ABROAD. HOW FAR DO I HAVE TO GO FOR FINANCIAL ADVICE?

For financial advice, who better to ask than the bank with more offices in more countries than any other UK clearing bank? Send off the coupon for more information about our range of expatriate banking services.

5/EH/9DEC

Please send me details of the Expatriate Advisory Service.

Name Mr/Mrs/Miss/Ms_____

Address_____

Country_____Postcode_____

Occupation_____

Employer_____

Nationality_____

Date of departure from/return to UK if applicable_____

Please return the coupon to either of the offices below. You may choose the island location to suit your personal preference.

Colin Freeman, Expatriate Services Manager, Barclays Bank PLC, Expatriate Services Centre, PO Box 9, Barclays House, Victoria Street, Douglas, Isle of Man. Tel: 0624 682244.

Gary Blake, Expatriate Advisory Officer, Barclays Bank PLC, Expatriate Department, PO Box 435, St. Helier, Jersey, Channel Islands. Tel: 0534 78511.

❀❀ **BARCLAYS OFFSHORE BANKING**

If, for example, the salary is denominated in British pounds, an exchange rate will be set once a year and the employee can choose the salary split that suits his requirements. This leaves the employee to profit or lose on the subsequent exchange movement until a new exchange rate is set at annual intervals.

Alternatively, a proportion of the salary will be paid locally but a reconciliation will be made every month or quarter to adjust the amount back to the home country equivalent. This will always ensure that the expatriate is never worse off in home country terms and any increases in local costs should be covered in his cost of living allowance.

Build-up method

A common approach combines the balance sheet system (see Chapter 7) with a currency split. An example of an Englishman working in Holland is shown below:

Home salary	£31,000
Less tax and social security	£7,452
Home net	£23,548

This is then broken into:

Home spendable (given in a table)	£16,816
Home savings	£6,732
Home payment	
Allowance for expatriation at 15%	£4,650
Home savings	£6,732
Subtotal	**£11,382**

Local payment
COLA index (from tables) 114
Exchange rate £1 = DFl4.35

Spendable income = Home spendable × COLA index × Exchange rate
= 16,816 × 1.14 × 4.35 = DFl83,390

In this example you assume that the company would provide housing and pay local taxes. Provided the exchange rate is reviewed every quarter, this method ensures that the expatriate has currency protection both in his home country and in the host country. As with any balance sheet approach the method depends on assumptions regarding average spending patterns provided by consultancy research but the calculation has a degree of internal logic.

High inflation countries

Expatriates can sometimes become trapped in high inflation countries, as in South America in the 1980s and perhaps the CIS in the 1990s. In these cases, a periodic adjustment of the balance sheet (every six months, for example) will not protect the expatriate from high local inflation. An additional mechanism is required – an inflation factor applied directly to the COLA. Take a situation where inflation is running at 120 per cent a year. Assuming that home-based inflation is negligible and currencies remained stable, it would be necessary to apply an increase of nearly 10 per cent on the COLA each month until such time as the whole balance sheet is formally re-adjusted.

Complexity, simplicity, security and risk

To a first-time expatriate, these currency considerations may appear dauntingly complicated. If you are operating in stable currency areas, you can safely ignore the problem, knowing that the total difference to your income will not vary much more than 5 per cent. However, if you choose to work in areas where exchange rates are volatile, and strict exchange controls operate, you would be well advised to understand any currency implications. No one wants to be stuck at the end of the assignment with a sackful of currency that cannot be repatriated. There is nothing more depressing than watching your initial fabulous salary dwindling in value so that in the end you can hardly meet your mortgage payments at home.

Well-established companies employing large numbers of expatriates will probably have worked out a measure of currency protection as explained above. Smaller organizations may not realize the implications to their half-dozen expats until complaints start coming back from the field. It is far better to have currency protection installed before you start your contract rather than trying to demonstrate hardship to the company at a later date.

10. Nasty Assignments

Many home-based employees view the expatriate as someone on a great deal who goes out to an easy-going job in a foreign country, works short hours and enjoys all the benefits of car, driver, servants and club – all at company expense. While his wife spends her days at coffee mornings or lazing around the pool, the children are packed away to expensive schools which the parents could never have afforded at home. In short, the expatriate is the classic fat cat who enjoys the best of everything but is always trying to extract a few more dollars from his long-suffering company.

The irony is that the widely held belief among expatriates is that all assignments are nasty – at least less nice than staying at home and that this should somehow be recognized as part of the compensation package. This may seem to be a dubious assumption, as expatriates tend to be a self-selecting group who may well revel in what others consider deprivations. However, there is no doubt that any expatriate assignment results in a degree of disruption and adjustment, if not exactly hardship. The most common problems associated with all expatriate assignments are:

- Adjustment at work to a different and often frustrating environment
- Disruption for the family concerning friends and neighbours
- Different climates, shopping patterns, entertainment etc
- The problem of learning (or sometimes not learning) a foreign language.

These are everyday hardships, encountered to some degree in nearly all expatriate assignments. Indeed, these are the areas frequently discussed during selection and briefing programmes as experience has shown that such minor aggravations can result in the failure of the expatriate and his family to stick with the assignment.

In most locations, it could be argued that there are plenty of compensations to balance out the negatives. Often the new home is grander, the expatriate manager has more status in the office than he had at home, climate and sports facilities may be better and there is a high-powered social life far removed from the expatriate's former surburban existence. Such are the attractions that some expatriates and their families can never properly re-adjust to their old domestic environment.

Niceness and nastiness for the expatriate is really a spectrum and rarely does one location have all the good things and another the nasty ones. Equally, one expatriate's paradise may well be another's hell depending on the perception of the posting. However, a random selection of nasty experiences might include:

- Traffic jams in Bangkok
- Violence in Nigeria
- Boredom in Geneva
- Illness in India
- Expense in Scandinavia
- Corruption in Indonesia
- Rudeness in France
- Altitude sickness in Bolivia.

Obviously, these are all clichés but they do encapsulate the main fears and phobias of the average expatriate. The US State Department, who go into the whole thing systematically, specify certain environmental factors when comparing a foreign location with the United States. They highlight:

- Isolation
- Climate and housing
- Food
- Education
- Importation
- Recreation
- Community facilities
- Altitude
- Natural hazards
- Sanitation
- Medical and hospital facilities
- Violence, crime and harassment.

This is a fairly comprehensive list and covers most aspects of nastiness. On closer examination, the problems with any foreign location can be grouped in four areas:

- 'Differences'

- Security
- Medical facilities
- Cultural isolation (and corruption).

Differences

Differences consist of aspects that are different from the home country but not necessarily better or worse.

The climate is an obvious one – hotter or colder, wetter or drier – but in the end it is all a matter of what you are used to. Recreation is another example – moving from Switzerland to Singapore might be great for a windsurfer but not so good for a skier. Social life, educational facilities and food can all be further examples – not necessarily better or worse, just different in the expatriate location.

Security

Security arrangements are usually pivotal in deciding what defines a nasty assignment. You may love the food, enthuse about the desert and relish 32 degrees in the shade, but no expatriate willingly exposes himself and his family to physical danger. The sense of physical danger is, of course, often heightened by the very fact of being in a strange place – a case could be made to an American that the murder rate in New York is higher than in, say, Lagos, Nigeria – but this is unlikely to reassure the expatriate and his family about security arrangements. Most fear of violence comes from the probability of robbery while at home or travelling. It is difficult to generalize but the occurrence of this sort of crime is high in certain African and South American countries. Most expatriates in these areas have their own horror stories regarding break-ins, physical assaults and, in rare cases, deaths of friends or colleagues. Most of the risk of robbery can be countered by employing security guards and living in compounds. Many houses in Africa are designed with high security cages around the sleeping accommodation – using the logic that any robbers will clean out the rest of the house but not bother breaking into the security cage. Away from the house, some countries have endemic problems with highway hold-ups – roadblocks set up especially after dark which make any travel out of the city extremely hazardous. In many countries, driving itself involves special kinds of danger. This can range from immediate imprisonment when involved in a road accident (frequent in the Middle East) to a lynch mob handing out rough justice to the driver who has hit a child in the road and was foolish enough to stop (not unknown in parts of Indonesia). This is in addition to the normal perils of the road whether it is a grand prix style driver in France or a logging truck in Malaysia.

All these factors add up to an increased sense of exposure to direct physical risk. A more subtle and insidious factor is a high level of harassment experienced in some countries. This may affect the expatriate in the work environment or more likely the family in everyday living.

Whether taking the form of aggressive begging or frequent appeals for petty bribes, the combined impression will be that of menace and harassment resulting in considerably higher levels of stress, if not any actual physical danger.

Medical facilities

Quite apart from fear of violence or accident, all expatriates are nervous about the efficiency of local medical facilities. This may be simply anxiety about communication difficulties but more often will be concern about the quality and sophistication of the services offered. The following situations may illustrate these concerns:

* * *

- An expatriate is waterskiing in a West African country. His finger is accidentally caught in the tow rope and nearly severed. He holds it together with a cloth and flies back to Europe rather than risk local infection or a blood transfusion.
- An international company provides full sterile 'up country' medical packs and organizes individual blood storage in all designated countries.
- There are two survivors of a plane crash in a remote island in Indonesia. One works for the local oil company and has a broken arm. The other works for an international oil service company and has severe injuries in the legs and chest. The oil service company charters a plane and 'medivacs' its employee to Singapore. After six months of intense treatment, he is well enough to return to the job. The 'lucky' local employee with only a broken arm was treated locally and died of secondary infection complications.

* * *

Large companies can often minimize the problems of medical facilities by providing their own company doctors (common in oilfield and construction camps) and developing fast and efficient medical evacuation arrangements. However, insecurity about local medical services will always be an expatriate concern – bad for the individual expatriate and multiplied many times over if a family is also resident.

Cultural isolation

Cultural isolation is the fourth group of hardships – really an extension of things being different but experienced in a more severe form. The absence of an expatriate community in the location will usually be viewed as a severe hardship, especially if integration into the local community is difficult. Particularly difficult languages – Japanese, Mandarin etc – can be very isolating for the average European or American. Working practices based on different premises from traditional western management methods may prove stressful:

* * *

- The expatriate in Africa designs an appraisal and promotion system based on merit only to discover that the system is never used. The locals strive to maintain a tribal balance (regardless of ability) to avoid eruption of intertribal violence.
- A manager in the Far East quickly discovers that all business is obtained by the payment of certain 'commissions' through an agent. If he is going to maintain a prosperous business he has no choice but to continue with the practice despite signing the head office ethical practice document each year.

* * *

Of course, cultural isolation cuts both ways but is often only viewed from a western perspective – the American learning a new language, the European dealing with corruption and nepotism. Hardship applies just as much to, say, an Asian or African coming to work in the US or Europe and encountering the weather, food and strange cultural habits of the locals. Inevitably, as most multinational companies are still predominantly western-oriented, they tend to view hardship through their own cultural spectacles.

In conclusion, it is fair to say that nearly all expatriates feel that the experience of working and living abroad is sufficient to be considered a hardship, despite snide comments to the contrary from their home-based colleagues. Apart from everyday inconveniences, security and medical facilities (or the lack of them) are most likely to top the poll when expatriates are asked to be specific about hardship. That brings us to a discussion of how hardship is measured and what, if anything, the company should do about it. This is dealt with in the next chapter.

11. Overseas Allowances

The previous chapter discussed nasty expatriate assignments, taking into account that there will always be an element of subjectivity in the definition of what exactly constitutes hardship. Clearly, the company has a responsibilty to ensure that it provides reliable security arrangements and adequate medical facilities and any other practical measures to minimize hardship for its employees. This approach can only go so far – after all, Nigeria still remains Nigeria, Indo-China will not change overnight etc – so that leaves the alternative of offering additional money to compensate for perceived hardship. Higher rewards will not make the locations any nicer but may make them easier to live with – a salary for suffering equation! When you discuss hardship with your employer, there are normally three ways in which this is recognized in terms of compensation.

Foreign service premium

The foreign service premium (FSP) is a common starting point for overseas allowances and may take the form of a percentage of base salary or a lump sum. With organizations operating only in developed countries this may be the only sort of incentive provided. For multinationals with a world-wide reach, the FSP may be the first layer of allowances, payable to all expatriates and then followed up with a series of hardship allowances based on specific locations. Frequently, if the incentive is based on a percentage of salary rather than a fixed sum, the applicable base salary will have a ceiling so that the incentive will only apply to a limited proportion of salary, eg the first £2000 of monthly salary.

It is difficult to give a precise range of FSPs but a 10–15 per cent range is normal, assuming, of course, the company accepts that all foreign assignments should offer some sort of premium. There has been a recent trend for some multinationals to drop FSPs altogether, partly to reduce costs, but also because they argue that working overseas is a natural part of any executive's career development – so why pay specially for overseas work?

Levels of hardship

The concept of levels of hardship is to measure and group locations and make appropriate incentive payments in each case. The problem is how this can be done when there is unlikely to be agreement on the exact nature of the hardship. The autocratic way is for management to decide, either on the basis of one person or a committee of senior managers with perhaps a review format built in each year. The disadvantage of this approach is that judgements are, by definition, associated with the management view of any location and therefore subject to criticism by expatriate employees. To avoid this, many companies use the services of an independent consultancy, both to give an aura of expertise and to shift the blame to someone else in cases of disagreement.

The usual consultancy approach to measuring hardship is to interview a cross-section of expatriates and construct a desirability rating for each location from their responses. Comparing this rating for a number of locations allows a ranking to be built up. Such an analysis can be given hardship weightings with, for example, security, medical facilities and cultural isolation as the three most important variables. Climatic conditions, food and recreation facilities might be judged as lesser factors carrying a smaller weighting. Each location being considered can then be scored against each factor using whatever weighting that has been agreed – a process very similar to points factor job evaluation. At the end of the analysis each location will receive a points total – the highest score being perceived as the least desirable location and the lowest score as the most desirable. If the company favours a more democratic approach, rather than using consultants, it can form an employee committee and make the same sort of hardship evaluation.

Types of payment

In practice, what is the general level of hardship payments and to what locations do they usually apply? Each company employing expatriates has its own particular list, and this may change over time as conditions and circumstances change. For most American and European companies high hardship payments are made where there is both a perceived security problem and local conditions are difficult. In this type of category, Libya, Nigeria, Central America and parts of Indo-China come to mind. To live in such locations, expatriates may well be offered a

70–100 per cent loading on their base salary. After these extremely high hardship postings, there is a mid range of locations in many parts of Africa, South America and Asia where some degree of hardship and/or security problem is identified. This could be Brazil, French West Africa, Beijing or even (given the pollution) Bangkok or Mexico City. Hardship payments in the range of 30–50 per cent are made to nearly all locations in the Middle East.

Usually hardship premiums are looked at from one cultural viewpoint. In reality, where the company has expatriates from a number of countries this approach is unfair. A European moving to another European country or a South American moving to another South American country will not experience the same degree of difficulty as when moving between continents. Alternatively, should an Indonesian moving to Aberdeen not receive an incentive similar to a Briton who works in Jakarta? This type of two-dimensional hardship is logical but a nightmare for any company to administer, and therefore rarely used in practice. Some companies do, however, use a concept of 'cultural zones' which result in lower hardship if you move within the zones and higher hardship payments if you move across zones. Typically, these zones would be:

- Europe, North America, Australasia
- South America
- Africa (excluding South Africa)
- Arab countries
- Asian countries (excluding Australia and China).

Such zones contain within them a number of anomalies. There is, for example, the language problem in Europe, tribal and racial differences in Africa and Asia etc. Nevertheless, the concept has some merit where organizations are widening their recruiting scope and want to remove the bias of an American or European perspective.

However hard the company tries, hardship and hardship allowances will always generate much disagreement and emotion. This is because it is a subjective matter which in the end can never be settled to everyone's satisfaction. Perhaps this is as it should be. What would the expatriate club be like if you could not enjoy a heated discussion about the merits and failings of locations round the world – and the stupidity of personnel administrators administering foreign service premiums!

12. Taxation

Benjamin Franklin said that the two inevitable things in life are death and taxes. While few would argue with this, the expatriate usually has to endure a rather more complex taxation situation than the average employee working in his home country. The very fact that you are not in your home country means that you will be faced with an alien tax regime, often with tax regulations in a foreign language and a tax bureaucracy even more impenetrable than the one you left back home. Moreover, when you accept an overseas contract the tax implications are bound to be something of a lottery. If one assignment sends you to Saudi Arabia and the other to Norway, the tax implications for your remuneration will vary tremendously.

Because of these factors the attitude of the employer towards an expatriate and tax payment is not the same as it is with the home-based employee. With the latter, tax payment is usually considered by the company to be a matter for the individual. Provided correct declarations and required stoppages are made, what happens between the tax authorities and the employee is a private matter. The expatriate, on the other hand, will often require a great deal of assistance with his tax problems and will usually expect a degree of company assistance in the payment of the tax bill in the country of assignment.

Different countries, different tax regimes

When a company is sending a number of expatriates to various locations round the world, its compensation specialists will try to build in a degree of equity in the way they structure the package. If all the intrepid travellers are being paid US$90,000 a year, Mr A in Sweden will be looking at a tax deduction of 65 per cent, Mr B in Brazil 33 per cent, Mr C in Hong Kong 14 per cent and Mr D in Oman 0 per cent. Moreover, each country will have different tax thresholds, marginal rates and tax on benefits. Even the European Community is a long way from harmonizing its income tax regimes. Clearly, this is totally unsatisfactory if you are on the receiving end, unless you ensure that your postings are exclusively to low tax countries – not an easy feat. Faced with the problem of expatriate tax payments, companies have devised a number of different approaches.

Individual tax responsibility

This is essentially the 'do nothing' approach, leaving the expatriate wholly responsible for paying tax in the host country. This will work well enough if you are coming from a high tax regime into a lower taxed environment. Provided you are given sufficient advice and assistance to fill in the declarations, tax payments will be less onerous than in the home country. However, this approach does not work if you are heading for a high tax regime unless the base salary is grossed up to compensate. Equally, there is no mechanism to establish equity in tax treatment between different locations. Not only will this make transfers difficult, it will probably engender a good deal of bad feeling from expatriates in different locations.

Tax protection

Tax protection implies that the expatriate will not pay more tax than he would have done in his own country on a comparable base salary. The calculation is usually made after the assignment tax bill has been paid and the expatriate can demonstrate that the tax take is higher than the home country tax would have been on his base salary. The company then pays the difference and any subsequent tax requirement.

* * *

Taking the example of an American working in Japan with a base of around US$100,000, tax protection (simply stated) would work like this:

Base salary: Y13.3 million
Taxable allowances: Y3.2 million
Housing: Y8 million
Vacation ticket: Y130,000
Education costs and miscellaneous items: Y260,000
Total taxable benefits: Y24,890
Tax rate @ 43% = Y10 million @ 130 = US$82,328

US tax based on salary of Y13.3 million (US$100,000) with allowances is, say, US$25,000. The company would therefore reimburse the employee US$57,890.

* * *

With tax protection, if the employee pays less tax in the host country than he would have done in his home country, he retains the difference.

Tax equalization

Tax equalization is similar to tax protection, only a little more sophisticated in its approach. Here the company has a policy that the expatriate will pay the equivalent tax that he would have paid on his base salary and bonus in his home country. This method fits in neatly with the balance sheet system (see Chapter 7) to the extent that it always takes the calculation back to the home country no matter what the prevailing rate of tax in the expatriate location. This means that each expatriate will be paying a rate equivalent to that of the country of origin. With a large number of expatriates the disadvantage is that tax equalization requires a lot of accountancy time and money to make the system work.

This is particularly true with US citizens, who have the misfortune to belong to a tax system that levies tax worldwide regardless of residency. Most countries in the world cease to tax their citizens when they are no longer resident, but Uncle Sam never lets you go, insisting on an annual tax return from wherever you are. Some companies will take a hard line and claim that home country tax liability is the responsibility of the individual.

* * *

This will hardly work for an American international company and here they will operate a tax equalization system of some complexity to equalize the net result of home and host country taxation. For example:

Base salary: US$100,000
Taxable allowances: US$50,000
Housing: US$50,000
Host country tax at 25% = US$50,000
US tax exclusion = US$70,000
Taxable amount therefore = US$130,000 at, say, 20% = US$26,000

The US expatriate therefore has a total tax bill of US$76,000.

If he were living in the States he would be taxed on the base salary of US$100,000 at, say, 18 per cent (claiming all his allowances) and would therefore pay US$18,000.

The company should therefore make a reimbursment of US$58,000.

* * *

This is a highly simplified example as the US tax system is complicated but it explains the essential concept of tax equalization. The advantage of the method is that it avoids any expatriate being penalized by a double tax system. The disadvantage is that it is complicated and can be expensive for the company, which may effectively be footing the bill for tax in two countries.

Tax pooling

A few international companies use the concept of a tax pool which applies a standard tax rate to all its expatriates. The approach is simple. The company will undertake to pay for all host country taxation wherever the expatriate is posted. It will then work out the average taxation percentage that applies to its expatriates worldwide. Thus the high figures from Scandinavia will be averaged out by the zero tax from the Middle East, ending up with an overall figure of perhaps 16 per cent. This rate will then be deducted from the base salary of all the expatriates. This type of approach works well when the company has a large number of expats all over the world and wants to treat them equally in tax terms. It has the added advantage of being self-funding as the deductions should roughly cover the tax demands. Tax pooling will, however, not help the American with his worldwide tax problem and will not fit in neatly with the balance sheet approach to remuneration.

Payment net of taxes

Some companies appear to avoid the complexity of the whole tax problem by paying all salaries net of taxes in the host country, on the surface offering the expatriate a tax-free deal. Usually, this type of approach is deceptive as some adjustment will have been made to the base salary to pay for the tax to be covered at company expense. It does have the advantage of putting the whole emotive issue into the hands of the accountant and giving a clear picture of the net worth of the package, but you may find returning to your home country and having to start paying tax again rather a shock under this system.

Everyone hates paying taxes. As one comedian said, the reward for energy, thrift and enterprise is ... paying more taxes! For many expatriates the advantage of their spell overseas is that they can earn high salaries and avoid paying high marginal tax rates. If they are lucky they can avoid paying any tax at all. The subject is, of course, an immensely complicated one which changes all the time as tax regulations round the world change. We hope this chapter has clarified a few of the issues and illustrated some approaches to the problems of expatriate tax. If you are a new expatriate there is no substitute for a careful study of the contract and detailed knowledge of your home country and host country tax regimes. Given patience and a little luck, you may find the foreign tax collector less burdensome than the domestic variety.

13. Pensions

Whether you are being transferred overseas by your current employer or taking a fixed-term contract with a new one, you will need to give some thought to the effect this could have on your pension rights, however tedious this might seem. Spending three or four years on assignment will undoubtedly affect your ultimate retirement income and you should try to understand the significance of any arrangements being made on your behalf. Unfortunately, only too often these arrangements are inadequate and you may wish to consider supplementing them through your own investment plans.

In so far as it is possible to evaluate what you will gain (or lose) from a pension arrangement, as an expatriate you should be aware that there are basically three approaches to be considered (four if you include not doing anything at all or making your own arrangements):

- Stay in a plan in your home country
- Enter a scheme in the country of assignment
- Move to an alternative international arrangement specifically designed for those on expatriate status.

Your freedom to choose between these alternatives will undoubtedly be restricted, partly because of the policies adopted by your employer and partly as a result of legislation which may make participation in certain government schemes a mandatory requirement.

Home country schemes

If you are able to remain in a plan in your home country, this is probably the least troublesome approach, especially if you are to be repatriated within a reasonable time. The basis for calculating contributions to and benefits from a home country scheme will usually be handled as a function of a notional salary reflecting what you would be paid if you were performing your overseas assignment in the home base. The notional salary is reviewed in the same way as actual salaries in the home country and, in theory, allows a smooth pay and pensions reintegration at the end of the assignment.

It was popular in the past, in some companies, to improve the value of the pension for staff working overseas by raising the multiplying factor on which benefits would ultimately be based or counting an extra year of service for each actual year spent on assignment. This is much less common today; there is no good reason why a pension benefit should be higher because of expatriate status.

Although a neat solution in some ways to pension continuity, the home country arrangement is not without its problems, especially when pension benefits are formed from the combination of occupational (ie company) and state administered schemes. While there are reciprocal agreements between certain countries which allow a great deal more flexibility, either to continue to contribute to the home country plan, or at least preserve home country rights while paying in the host location, this is certainly not always the case. Often a short period of mandatory participation in the host country's state scheme will be insufficient for the contributor to qualify for a pension benefit on retirement and the payments made, probably by the employee and the company, are frequently a waste of money. In some cases, compulsory withdrawal from the home country state scheme may also lead to an eventual reduction in pension entitlement.

Another disadvantage of remaining in the home country scheme is revealed if the employee stays overseas for any significant period. Apart from the fact that he may not be able to remain in the scheme indefinitely (certainly the case for UK-based employees – ten years is the absolute maximum if employed by a subsidiary of a UK company), the value of the accumulated benefits may also become increasingly inadequate if he intends to retire away from the home base.

There may also be significant tax disadvantages in remaining in the home country scheme. Participation may be tax efficient while living in the home base where employee contributions are tax deductible, since tax will only be due when the retirement income is paid; while living overseas, employee deductions are often not considered as tax deductible in the local tax regime and the advantage is therefore lost if the employee eventually retires in the home base. In some countries (Japan, for example), the local tax authority may regard the employer's contribution as a taxable benefit in the hands of the employee.

Assignment country schemes

Assignment country schemes should only be considered if the employee will remain in the location long enough to ensure that he has a right to the benefits available and if there is some freedom to transfer accumulated assets in the assignment country plan back to a home country scheme. Sometimes this is not possible – again, Japan has legislation which makes it virtually impossible. If you are planning to stay in the assignment country indefinitely, it is also important to determine whether or not accumulated funds in a home country scheme can be imported to build up a better eventual retirement income in what may become your new home base.

Some home country plans are worth entering. France, for example, operates schemes supplementing state programmes which are generous on retirement because the pension rights earned each year are revalued using a point-based formula which ensures that increases in the cost of living are factored into the eventual retirement benefit. These schemes also sometimes invest the contribution received in luxury resort complexes which can be used by both active and retired scheme members at low rents.

Host country plans also have the advantage of integrating with any mandatory local state schemes, though this may ultimately create problems if the assignment is relatively short.

Pensions and the European Community

With the greater freedom of movement within European Community (EC) countries since 1992, the existing flexible reciprocation rules on state pension scheme participation will become increasingly important. Under certain circumstances (normally short-stay assignments of less than one year), it is possible to continue in a home country state plan when the move is between two EC countries. Even when participation in the host EC country's scheme is mandatory, the rules governing eventual pension benefit payment ensure that employment in a number of Community countries, during a working life, is not made unattractive by the erosion of pension rights. The procedures which govern these reciprocal arrangements are complicated, however, and specialist guidance should be sought from local bodies governing social security programmes within the relevant member countries.

Apart from the issues surrounding EC countries, it is sometimes advisable to maintain contributions to a home country state pension scheme, even when the alternative arrangements made by your employer are reasonably attractive. This is certainly the case for UK nationals when they are able to make relatively cheap Class 3 scheme contributions to ensure that their basic state pension is adequately secured. Measured in terms of a return on investment, the payback is generally considered to be good value for money. Many companies will also actively encourage this discipline, and will go to great lengths to allow their employees to participate, since their philosophy will be to keep the employee 'whole' in both the company and state programmes of the home country. This is common with US employers and the FICA (Federal Insurance Contribution Act) government scheme.

International plans

Some companies operate pension plans which are separate from those available in the home or host countries. Loosely defined as international plans, they are usually designed around two major considerations:

- Third country nationals, joining the company as expatriates from a country other than the one in which the parent is based, may not have the privilege of a home base plan on which to depend. If they are unable to join the HQ country's scheme, or there is no point in going into the host country plan, because of the problems of mobility described on page 74, an international 'catch all' approach is a logical alternative.
- Employees, moving between various home-based and expatriate locations during a career, often accumulate a rag-bag of pension rights from different state and company schemes around the world – especially when they move between a parent company and its acquired divisions where there tend to be different schemes. Some companies respond to this by setting up an 'umbrella' international scheme which ensures that, after all the various pension rights around the world have been determined, a further, supplementary entitlement is available as protection should the total benefit fall short of a predetermined minimum level based on the employee's length of service.

There is a third form of international plan offered by those companies where staff are required to be highly mobile and are drawn from a wide variety of different countries. In this case, the employer uses a simple worldwide plan for all international staff which becomes the principal arrangement even when employees are assigned to the home base. These plans tend to ignore state pension benefits which might accumulate on the basis that, because of the mobility requirement, they are rarely realizable anyway.

Companies unable to guarantee long-term employment sometimes establish a deferred income plan as an alternative (or an additional) benefit to retirement income. Often termed a provident fund, this usually involves setting aside an amount of money each year, calculated as a percentage of current salary, which is then invested and the proceeds paid to the employee when the company can no longer provide employment – or at the end of a predefined contract period. This payment may also be used to satisfy any entitlement the individual may have to redundancy or severance benefits in the home base country or the last employment location.

Because they are not tied to the regulations of a single country, international retirement or deferred income plans are often funded in offshore tax havens to minimize tax liabilities and to ensure a flexible investment strategy. Where the benefits are not integrated into pension rights which may have been acquired from other schemes, employers may give members a limited right to choose how investments are handled.

The benefit formulae used vary enormously and may either generate a guaranteed pension which is a function of the employee's last earnings and the number of years of service or it may be in the form of a simple lump sum cash payment. The maximum payment available is often determined in the same way as it would be under the local scheme in the parent company's headquarters location.

Offshore funds are also sometimes used as part of a pension planning arrangement for countries where the accrual of funds in that location would give rise to an unacceptably high tax liability, either for the company or the employee. In order to avoid this, the company simply promises to pay the employee the prescribed benefits, without establishing a formally recognized pension scheme in that country, and sets up an offshore fund which exactly 'mirrors' the value of any promised benefits.

These reasonably clear-cut strategies may give the impression that expatriate pension planning can always be handled rationally. The reality is often quite the opposite. In order to provide a highly organized, fully integrated scheme, a company will normally require a large investment in staff and administration: few companies are willing to make this a high priority in the belief that the cost and the effort are not justified. They take the view that, since most expatriates find it difficult to understand anything other than the most basic concepts of pension arrangements, there is not a great deal to be gained.

From your point of view, it is nevertheless worthwhile to try to find out where you stand. The simplest approach is to ask questions, at the early stages of negotiation, which will allow you to determine whether or not the overseas assignment will ultimately cause an erosion in the level of pension entitlement that you would expect to receive if you were to remain in the home base. If you are convinced that you will not suffer – fine. If this is not the case, you may wish to talk about the possibility of an international supplementary plan, a lump sum, a compensatory payment or a higher salary level than the one on offer. While the subject of pensions may, in itself, be tedious to the majority of people, it can sometimes be used as a powerful negotiating tool in obtaining the most favourable terms for an overseas appointment.

Finally, when you have negotiated the best deal you can obtain regarding your pension, you must then incorporate the situation into your own financial planning. If you have not managed to obtain pension rights while overseas, it will be necessary to plan more carefully how you save any discretionary income as a result of the assignment. After all, pensions are only a form of deferred income – there is nothing to stop anyone making their own arrangements. This is discussed more fully in Chapter 22.

14. Accommodation

Few subjects exercise even the most hardened expatriates more than where they will live. You should not leave home without a clear idea of where your next home will be. If the issues surrounding accommodation are not spelled out in straightforward terms, arguments and frustration will drag on for many months into the assignment.

Key questions on housing

As a minimum, you should get answers to the following before you accept an appointment:

- Am I paying for any of it?
- If I am, what is my share and what impact will it have on my salary?
- Do I choose where I live or will I be told to move into a property already owned/leased by the employer?
- If I can choose, is there a guideline on price and is it fair in relation to my peers?
- Is accommodation a taxable benefit and who will pay the tax which might arise?
- What happens to my accommodation at home? Does my package assume that I will maintain it or is this all part of the great adventure of living overseas?
- Who arranges the lease and makes payments? Are there property taxes to pay, and if so who pays? Are there up-front costs (deposits, rental advances, agent's fees), and if so who pays?
- Assuming there is a cash sum available for accommodation, can I choose to buy rather than rent and is there any help with purchase/sale costs?
- Who pays for heating, air-conditioning, telephone etc?

Company subsidized accommodation

Decisions about who pays for what will usually be determined by global company policies. These may range from the employee looking after everything (much more typical in the United States and many European countries), through complex housing allowances designed to compensate for the differences in costs in the home base and the host country (difficult to administer when employees converge from Bangladesh and Switzerland), to everything being paid for and settled by the company, possibly with a contribution from the employee's salary package. (This is more common in less developed countries where the whole process of finding a home can be horrendous.)

The cost of utilities (electricity, gas, telephone etc) can be particularly high in some countries and many companies recognize this with some form of compensation. Where pay packages have a component which reflects the relative differences in costs of living between two countries, it is common for utility charges to be factored into any premium which is to be paid. Others arrange a special allowance for this purpose or pay the bill directly on the employee's behalf where this is tax efficient. Whatever system is used, your employer will normally expect you to make some form of contribution towards the cost. Without this, expenses can go through the roof (literally, in the case of heating bills). Some expatriate families become totally irresponsible with the company's money, leaving heaters or the air-conditioning on all day and night whether or not they are in the house.

The employer's concerns

To help you come to terms with what is on offer, and make the most of any available flexibility, it is worth considering what is uppermost in the minds of most employers on this subject:

- The sooner the employee and family move out of a hotel and into permanent accommodation the better. A family of four consumes a vast amount of money in room charges, meals, laundry bills etc – about £350–£450 a day in most major centres (and whatever the company is planning to pay towards permanent housing, it is not, typically, £12,000 a month). By minimizing the time spent in temporary accommodation, you will not only save the company money, but also show a willingness to become fully productive quickly. This may improve your chances of extracting a little more cash towards permanent housing or furnishings.
- Many tax authorities allow favourable tax treatment for accommodation provided directly by the employer. In Hong Kong, for example, housing is taxed as a flat 10 per cent of the declared income,

regardless of the cost of the rental. It is useful to be aware of this when comparing net pay in the home base and the host location.

- By allowing you too much freedom of choice, the employer may be left with the legacy of an unlettable or unsaleable house when the assignment ends. Leases are inconvenient (and usually binding) agreements and an efficient employer will be keen to ensure that yours expires or can be taken over by somebody else when you move on. Knowing this will help you to understand why there are often so many limitations on what you are allowed to do. It may not help you to negotiate a better deal but, by being aware of it, you will come to terms more easily with what is on offer.

- It is worth knowing that the actual rental paid is not always the real cost. For example, when the housing market is depressed, landlords are often keen to maintain a relatively high monthly rental but will be willing to offer unseen savings in the form of rental 'holidays' (ie no payment) for several months or a cash contribution towards fitting out an apartment or house. Always make sure that any advantage secured in this way is taken into consideration when your entitlement is being fixed.

Cash allowances

Many employers avoid the outwardly attractive option of providing employees with a monthly cash sum to do with as they please. Problems of reletting unsuitable accommodation to a subsequent employee when staff leave, and the additional difficulty of policing the allowance when rent levels rise, are the main reasons for shunning this approach. There is also the point that you are representing the public face of the company in what is often a highly impressionable, close-knit community. Is the image that you are presenting in a third-rate lodging house behind the railway station one that suits the organization?

Purchasing property

Many companies will want to avoid the pitfalls of allowing you to buy property, however attractive the short-term gains may be in an apparently buoyant housing market. While the tax relief on housing loan interest may help to improve the net value of a package, the drawbacks for the employer tend to outweigh the positive aspects. Apart from managing the imponderables of how much to give and how much to adjust when prices change, there is going to be an asset to be disposed of when the assignment ends, often a huge millstone and usually around the company's neck rather than the employee's. The last thing anybody needs, when the supposedly mobile assignee is due to leave, is a protracted house sale. Nor will the employer want to become involved with your problems exporting cash brought into the country for the purpose of house purchase which has been substantially eroded in value by an unfavourable fluctuation in exchange rates.

What the well-organized company will offer

You will find that many are not well organized but it is worth knowing what to ask for. At least you can form an opinion about how you will be dealt with by the answers you receive:

- Unless the company owns accommodation, a reputable property agent (or a member of the company's staff) should be available immediately upon your arrival, not only to help you find somewhere to live but also to help with lease arrangements, furniture inventories, connecting utilities etc.
- A clear statement showing the limits on what you can spend should be communicated. This may be in the form of a matrix relating to your job grade and family status (see below for an example).

Expatriate rental cost ceilings
(in currency per month)

Grades	Single/married no children	Married + one	Married + two etc
14/15	500	600	700
12/13	400	500	600
10/11	300	400	500
8/9	200	300	400

Whatever the system, it should ensure parity with colleagues and be fairly and consistently applied.

- Up-to-date and well-researched information about what is on offer should be available before the assignment commences. What are the typical dimensions? What facilities are available? How far is it from the office and school and what kind of commute can be expected? Is there any public transport nearby? Maps showing locations and photographs of typical properties should be on offer to give the employee and his family the sense of being able to plan from a distance.
- There should be a clear policy dealing with property in the home

base. Some companies are unwilling to take responsibility for looking after this though most balance sheet based remuneration philosophies recognize that the cost exists. Help with leasing arrangements, if you decide to let out the house you own, is an increasingly common benefit. Assistance may be in the form of paying for a lawyer to draw up a water-tight tenancy agreement or a contribution towards property management fees. Alternatively, reimbursing all or part of the selling costs is frequently offered (though subsidizing purchase costs on return at the end of an assignment is not always guaranteed). Paying lease-breaking penalties of up to three months' rental is a fairly standard practice when the employee is not a home owner in the home base.

- Although a number of companies consider it an unnecessary expense, a visit to the assignment location (with or without the spouse) can often shorten the process of searching for the right home. It can also put employees off the idea of making the move even before they have had a chance to come to terms with it, but, in practice, this rarely happens.

- A diplomatic clause in the lease, even if it means paying slightly over the going rate, will be considered essential by the employer who insists on as much flexibility as possible for a mobile workforce. This is an escape route which lets the lessee out of the tenancy agreement, usually after the first 12 months, because the employee has to be transferred to another country. It can even be used to break the contract when the employee simply wants to live somewhere else in the same city, though this may not always be within the accepted meaning of the clause. It could be embarrassing to meet your landlord, several months after moving, if he thought you were leaving the country.

In some ways, one has to be a cynical idealist on the subject of expatriate housing, living in constant hope that the policy will fulfil its promise but accepting, at the same time, that the sum of the parts of what is promised on paper rarely becomes an acceptable whole.

15. Spouses and Partners

Many of the more rigorous expatriate assignments are referred to as single-status appointments. Families do not usually accompany the workers to oil rigs in the jungle or desert construction sites. Some cultures take the concept of single-status expatriation even further. The Japanese expatriate is often sent overseas for several years on single status, while his family stays in Japan together with most of the salary and benefits. However, for many western companies, the overseas posting is for the employee and his family. The feasibility of accepting an overseas assignment largely depends, for most couples, on three crucial factors:

- Is there enough information available to make a decision about whether they both want to go?
- Is it worth the possible loss of one income and the sacrifice of one partner's career for the opportunities and advantages on offer?
- What is the company's position on common law spouses and couples living together during an assignment?

Preparation

If the spouse has not been fully informed about what to expect, he or she may build a completely false set of expectations and perceptions about the assignment. The more that can be done to give a realistic picture of life in the new location, the greater the chance of the assignment being successful. Briefing spouses is a matter of the company ensuring that material relevant to the wife or husband is made available and that the spouse is included in a face-to-face briefing held either by the employer or an external organization. It is helpful to provide the spouse with contacts, both within and outside the company, on arrival in the new location. While it may be easy to blame the employer for not doing enough in this area, it is still crucial for you, the employee, to do something about it if the employer is not providing enough help.

Dual career problems

The issue of dual income/dual career families is becoming increasingly important as the movement towards equal opportunities in the workplace gathers momentum. What can you reasonably expect from your employer on this issue if it affects you? If you are one of several candidates for a post, and you expect some financial compensation for the fact that your spouse is sacrificing his or her job, it will almost certainly not be forthcoming. Even if you are the only available person for a key post, it is unlikely that money will be granted specifically for this reason, though an invisible premium may be added into the package as a sweetener to make the deal more attractive. As things stand, most couples come to terms with the financial issue on the basis of what is usually a significant improvement in at least one income and the opportunity to swap career aspirations, at least temporarily, for the pleasures of expatriation. Employers will largely ignore this issue as long as there is a pool of suitable individuals for whom the concept of two incomes is not relevant.

This is not to say that the employer should not make an effort to help the spouse make a good career move in the new location. Employees may expect some help on this in the form of circulating the spouse's details among suitable local contacts and arranging for pre-assignment language lessons where necessary. Occasionally, they may even pay for a local outplacement organization to help with finding a job or pay for retraining, though this is rare. It is also worth the employee asking if there are jobs available with the employer in the country of assignment – an obvious solution, but one that is frequently overlooked.

In situations where the work location and the home base are geographically close, there is an increasing tendency for the couple to live apart so that the spouse can continue with his or her career. Companies are gradually introducing more flexible cash-based compensation policies which will allow the employee to spend less on building comfortable surroundings in the host location and more on reunion air fares and maintaining two households. This is also an issue for established families who, for perfectly amicable reasons, prefer to live apart – for example, for the sake of the children's education – with only the employee living in the work location. Companies are increasingly accepting the reality of this situation, though there are the hidden risks of the employee becoming isolated and withdrawn through living for a prolonged period outside the context of the immediate family.

Unmarried couples

Employers agonize over the problems associated with couples who are not married claiming the same status as those who are. Views tend to polarize on the moral issue. There are those who claim that the company has no right to judge and that, if a reasonable definition of cohabitation can be established on the lines of legislation in the Netherlands and Australia where the concept of the *de facto* marriage is now an acceptable norm, this should apply to all established partnerships. At the other end of the scale, some companies feel that they have the right to recognize only legally constituted permanent arrangements and that they should not be asked to condone what, until quite recently, was considered to be immoral behaviour.

In reality, of course, there are many practical considerations which are more important than the moral ones:

- However much a company may want to take an enlightened view on unmarried relationships, many countries will not grant entry visas to spouses unless a marriage certificate can be produced. This may effectively bar the partner from accompanying the employee and it is not a problem restricted to countries such as Saudi Arabia; entering the United States for any length of time, as anything other than a married dependant, can be extremely difficult.
- Assuming the unmarried partner is able to enter the country through his or her own efforts, it may be impossible for the couple to share property because of local laws. Even if this is legal, the practice of a couple living together may be so unacceptable that the friction which arises, both in the social and business communities, may be too great to make such a move practical.
- The prospects for unmarried couples are undoubtedly less attractive than for those who have chosen to legalize their relationship. However, this should not prevent them from attempting to pursue either single or dual careers outside their country of origin. Despite the legal and cultural restrictions, some companies try to take an enlightened view, even though they may limit the degree of assistance to those who can prove that they have lived together for a minimum number of years – or decide simply on the evidence of each case as it arises.

Marital stress and expatriation

The additional stress placed on a marriage (or an unmarried relationship for that matter) is a much probed aspect of expatriate life. Neither the spouse nor the employee should be under any illusion that moving to another country will help to rescue an already foundering relationship. If anything, it will speed up the process of separation. There are usually too many distractions and new pressures and too few opportunities to run temporarily to the safety and comfort of close family and friends.

To expand on this issue would be to stray into the field of marriage guidance – which is not the purpose of this book. Assuming your relationship with your spouse is reasonably stable, it should be necessary only to examine the following, fairly obvious but sometimes neglected, questions when considering a move overseas:

- Is it what you both want? Or is there a strong possibility that a less willing partner will continually use the cry of 'I didn't want to come in the first place. You made me!' as a point of argument in future quarrels?
- Are either of you so reliant on close friends and relatives at home, as a refuge and support when friction arises between you, that their unavailability will prevent you from being able to unburden all the anger and frustration which builds up before a damaging domestic crisis?
- Do you both have the same vision about how and when the assignment should end? In other words, do you both expect to come back to your country of origin after three years and return to the same domestic life or is one partner looking for an open-ended adventure which might lead anywhere?
- Are your expectations of the lifestyle and environment in the country of assignment broadly the same? If one party is intent on recreating the suburban existence of the home country while the other is looking for an opportunity to experience a completely different, probably more exotic, way of life, it will not be too long before you are at each other's throats.

A final word on fiancés. Many companies will take a sympathetic view about your intention to marry when you tell them at the time you are offered a posting abroad, particularly if you can convince them that this was your intention even before the opportunity arose. While they may not always be willing to pay for you to return to your home base for the wedding, they will usually commit themselves to paying relocation and accommodation costs which reflect your forthcoming married status.

16. Kids, Pets and Other Animals

This chapter deals with all the expatriate's dependants (in various forms) other than the spouse. Since issues relating to schooling are covered in Chapter 17, this chapter addresses a number of points relating to children, and dependants in a broader sense, during the assignment. In addition, since many people treat their pets as though they were dependants, it is both appropriate and convenient to deal with these two forms of life under one heading.

A definition of dependent children

One of the biggest headaches faced by personnel managers is the task of trying to define whether or not a child should be recognized as a dependant during an assignment. It is worth examining the problem from the employer's viewpoint.

When an expatriate and spouse have their own children, and they accompany their parents on the assignment, everything is straight-forward – schooling policies, size of accommodation, shipment of personal effects and other allowances determined by the number of accompanying offspring are easy to calculate.

It becomes more difficult when either parent introduces children from a previous marriage. Further complications arise when the employee or the spouse has children living with a previous wife or husband in another country and there is still some financial dependence on the assignee. Does the company pay for reunion trips, accommodation, schooling costs etc?

* * *

Some expatriates make life very complicated. Take the case of the executive who was originally based in the UK. He is on his second marriage and there are two children as a result of this relationship. His wife has brought one child to the union from a previous marriage and this child is now legally adopted by the employee. He also has a child from his first marriage, living with his first wife, whom he must continue to support since his first wife has not found a new partner. How does the employer decide who is a dependant and who is not?

*   *   *

Most companies tend to recognize accompanying children who are legally adopted by the employee and who depend on him entirely for financial support. While the definition of legal custody may vary from country to country, this is a reasonably broad yardstick. Where dependent children from a previous marriage are not living with the employee, help with reunion air fares and accommodation space for visits is frequently provided but not schooling costs or allowances related specifically to the assignment location.

Children from a spouse's previous marriage, who are in the custody of the spouse's first husband or wife, are difficult cases. Normally, nothing more than a reunion trip is provided though some companies are more generous. You will find that most employers try to resolve these problems with great care and sensitivity, realizing that their employees may resent any encroachment on their personal lives, particularly when it concerns failures and disappointments from the past. However, you will find that only so much individual flexibility can be offered. A precedent set with one family will invariably give rise to a string of similar claims from others.

Employees with grown-up children present another set of difficulties. When do they cease to be dependent? Typically, companies will recognize offspring over the age of 18 if they are still in full-time education up to the age of 21. While they are accompanying parents during the assignment, in this age group they usually count when calculating family-size related expatriate benefits (excluding schooling costs if they are in post-secondary education). If they remain in the home base, reunion air-fare provision is common.

Children born overseas

While some families bring children with them to the assignment, others produce new ones while they are there. A number of issues arise related to giving birth during an overseas assignment and these are covered in Chapter 18. One non-medical point which must be considered is the question of nationality. It is often extremely important to think carefully about having children while away from the home base since there is a chance that they will not be granted citizenship at home.

* * *

An Indian couple who emigrated to Canada and became naturalized citizens discovered that they were expecting a baby during an assignment to Singapore. On checking with the immigration authorities in Canada, they learned that, if they wanted their child to be given the right to Canadian citizenship, it would have to be born in Canada. Fortunately, the pregnancy was not too far advanced and the mother-to-be was able to fly back to Toronto in time for the birth.

* * *

Many companies will take a sympathetic view of this type of problem and assist with the cost of air fares and temporary accommodation.

There are other measures relating to nationality which should be considered when having children in another country. Always ensure that the child's birth has been adequately registered with the appropriate home country embassy or consulate in the work location. There are often specific procedures for handling this task which should not be overlooked in the post-birth excitement. It is also wise to obtain a passport for the new child as soon as possible; registering the child on one or both of the parents' passports is the recommended practice but it is so much easier to give children flexibility to travel independently, in the event of an emergency, by ensuring that they have their own documentation. (This might arise, for example, if both parents are ill and it is necessary for a child to travel back to the home base with a grandparent.)

Since birth certificates of children born overseas are not always easily obtainable in later life, parents who obtain several copies at the time of the birth registration will be acting with great foresight.

Other dependants

Apart from offspring, what position do most companies take on other (human) dependants such as grandparents and relatives who live permanently with an employee in the home base? The answer is usually nothing – at least formally in policy terms – since this gives rise to a multitude of problems (visas, accommodation, repatriation – dead or alive – to name but a few). Concessions are occasionally made; for example, when a key employee categorically refuses to take an assignment unless his mother can come with him.

Pets

The biggest problem, of course, is moving an animal to a new location and then trying to repatriate it at the end of the assignment. Children, in this respect, are much easier to handle. Companies are divided about equally between those who agree to pay for and help with the transportation of animals and those who believe that it is better to have nothing to do with this problem.

The expenditure for the relocation of animals falls into the following categories:

- *Preparation of documentation.* This will include the transportation arrangements, certificates of health and immunization.
- *Vaccinations and health checks.* Most countries have strict regulations and it is essential to ensure that your pet is adequately protected against illnesses which may not be common in the home base.
- *Transportation.* Somebody must take the animal through the formalities at the airport and on to the plane. A suitable cage must be prepared in the cargo hold and adequate provision made for food and water during an extended journey. At the other end, an agent may be required to handle another set of formalities for entering the new country.
- *Quarantine periods.* Some countries have a mandatory period of quarantine when the animal must be boarded away from its owners to ensure that there is no evidence of rabies or similar dangerous and contagious diseases. The UK is usually cited as an example of this practice where a six-month quarantine period is required. This is an expensive and often emotionally upsetting process for the family and many pets (and families) never recover from the experience.

* * *

A devoted pet owner accepted his first expatriate assignment from Australia to Hong Kong. The family moved from Sydney to one of the few house-with-garden residences in Hong Kong so that the dog could feel at home. Unfortunately, owing to business conditions, the assignment terminated after six months. The pet-loving family then discovered that, in order to get the pet back to Sydney, it had to be quarantined in either Hawaii, Japan or the UK. Worse still, the travel-weary pet would not actually get home for nine months! Sad to relate, the pooch never made it, expiring in some far-off Hawaiian kennel. The family got a new dog, but they never became expatriates again.

* * *

Agents can often be appointed to handle the whole process. However, the embassy of the work location, the airline carrying the pet and possibly specialist animal associations should be consulted if you plan to handle it all yourself.

Once safely in the new country, it is essential that you find out what 'dos and don'ts' of pet ownership must be observed. In Britain, for example, a dog licence is required. In other countries, the wearing of flea collars for cats and dogs is mandatory. Elsewhere, it may be unwise to allow a pet to roam unleashed in the streets; it might be impounded or even eaten. In tropical countries, dogs often suffer abominably from the heat and from parasites and other irritating local wildlife which will cause considerable distress unless regular veterinary checks are carried out.

A sad story from a family based in the Far East who acquired a pet rabbit which they kept in a cage in the house. In order to control local pests such as termites, white ants and cockroaches, they had an agreement with a local contractor who periodically sprayed the inside of the house with the necessary chemicals. While the contractor gave plenty of warning about keeping children outside during the spraying, he forgot to mention pets and the rabbit suffered an unpleasant death after inhaling the chemicals.

17. Education

For expatriates with dependants, this is probably the second biggest headache after finding somewhere to live. Happy, well-adjusted children are one of the keys to a stable family life and this is even more true during an overseas assignment. Children who move from country to country with their parents are, at best, adaptable and more knowledgable about the world than their counterparts who stay at home; at worst, they become members of an international brat-pack, often finding it difficult to settle in an adult world with no servants or bottomless money supplies to sustain them.

For some children, expatriate life will never be suitable and this is going to be one of the fundamental issues when considering an assignment. While a few countries are well equipped to deal with handicapped or psychologically disturbed children, this is rarely going to be an easy path to follow and should only be pursued after a great deal of serious thought. It may be possible to cope with the stresses and anxieties in a familiar setting, but they can rapidly become overwhelming when combined with the new frustrations and fears of strange and often hostile surroundings on the other side of the world.

Preparation

Assuming that your children are going to be able to adjust, the first requirement is information about the schooling options available. The best employers will provide copious briefing material and will answer your questions with endless patience. At an early stage in the run-up to the move, you should obtain prospectuses on the schools available and contact addresses for making your initial approaches. However superficial this information may be, it will at least give you something to evaluate and allow your children to picture their new surroundings.

You should also put forward the argument that you would like to evaluate the schools at first hand (and even register your children) as a justification for a pre-assignment visit to the location. School and eventual home are inextricably linked and it is often practical to tie these two items up at the same time. In many countries, there are waiting lists for entry and debentures to be purchased. To turn up with your children, hoping for instant acceptance, is just not going to work. Try to find out what the position is and, as a minimum, have your children registered well in advance of your departure.

If the process of securing a place in a school is particularly difficult, or a face-to-face interview is a prerequisite for acceptance, you could suggest that your children accompany you on the pre-assignment visit. Not many companies will agree readily to this but they may at least agree to help with some of the costs if it will guarantee a smooth entry and minimize the risk of the assignment failing.

If there is any flexibility on your commencement date, you should plan to start the assignment at the beginning of the school holidays. In most countries, this would be in July or August (though in Australia and New Zealand it would be January). Your children will then be able to finish school at the end of term in the home country, become acclimatized in their new surroundings for several weeks and begin the new school year with everybody else – much better than being dumped into a classroom in mid-term when every other child has already settled into the school routine. Since others are thinking in the same way, in the larger expatriate communities this may also give you the advantage of a wider selection of available housing; departing expatriates will be moving out at this time of the year.

You should also ask to be put in touch with people already in the location with school-age children. This is probably one of the best ways to obtain a reasonably objective assessment of what is available. It also gives you social contacts with other parents and your children will have some support in the playground on the first day at school.

If you have the opportunity, you should also try to organize some pre-assignment, local language training. Even where international schools are available, and the local language is not the normal medium of teaching, this can be a confidence booster, especially when the local language is part of the school curriculum.

On the subject of language training, it is wise to ask your employer, during your initial discussions, whether or not tuition in your home country language is available while on assignment (and who will pay for it). Your children are unlikely to forget how to speak their mother tongue since you will obviously use it at home. However, they may rapidly fall behind the academic standards in their home country and this could present serious problems on your eventual repatriation.

Schooling options

Types of schooling obviously vary enormously around the world. If you are moving from a European country or from the USA to a major city, your children should normally be able to continue in an education system similar to the one at home – if your employer or you are willing to pay.

International schools

International schools, catering for US, British, French, Dutch or German children are fairly common both at primary and secondary levels. Standards of teaching are generally high since there is competition among teachers to spend some time overseas and the school authorities can pick the best. Problems of discipline tend to be minor and a great deal of parent–teacher contact is common because of the size and nature of the expatriate community. This is not to say that conditions are always ideal. There have been problems with drug abuse and absenteeism. Moreover, because the schools operate fairly independently, they do not necessarily pursue a curriculum which matches the standards and requirements of the home country.

Boarding schools

If suitable schooling is not available in the work location, or you expect to move through assignments in a number of different countries, the option of a boarding school in the home base is worth considering. This is particularly relevant to UK-based expatriates but there are also boarding schools in North America and in other European countries. Apart from the obvious considerations of family separation and the perception you may have about these schools, you will also need to bear in mind the expense of reunion air fares, what to do about weekends and shorter holidays, and the future decision about whether you can afford to pay the fees when you eventually return – possibly at a critical point in your child's education.

Local state schools

Local schools are probably only worth considering at nursery or primary level or where the local language is the same as in the home country. Despite this, many company policies dictate that, if suitable free local secondary schooling is available, it should be used. This is always a vexing issue: by what standards does one define suitable? The company in the location may feel that local facilities are perfectly adequate; you will probably think otherwise. As a result, this type of policy is sometimes ignored when there are more 'suitable' international schools available.

Costs

The biggest question, of course, is what costs do most companies pay? At present rates, a fully-tax protected reimbursement of all costs would, typically, leave little change out of £6000–£7000 each year per child at senior international school level, probably much more for boarding schools or for most US schools overseas.

Generally speaking, school fees for suitable schools for the dependants of accompanying family members are paid at primary and secondary levels by the majority of large, multinational employers. In some cases, a small contribution is required from the employee. A few, more generous, organizations pay for everything including books and materials, uniforms and transportation costs to and from school – despite the fact that these are usually borne by the parents when living in the home base. The extent to which your employer provides full or partial reimbursement will have to be evaluated in the context of the total package offered. You may expect, but you are unlikely to be given, the best of everything. Generous treatment on schooling costs, for example, may well be combined with less favourable housing arrangements.

Another concern will be the age from which schooling costs are met by the employer. Since nursery school/kindergarten costs are more frequently borne by parents rather than by the state in the home location, it is relatively unusual for companies to pay all pre-primary school expenses. While primary school costs are often paid from the term in which a child reaches the age of five, this may not be the case with an American employer whose global policy will often reflect the fact that first grade in junior school in the USA is for six-year-olds.

Where boarding school costs are met by the employer, it is common to pay for secondary school level only. Since the boarding school option means that the parents are able to reduce their costs in the work location (less food, heating, air-conditioning etc), companies frequently place a cap on the amount they will reimburse either by establishing an absolute maximum payment or by paying only a percentage of the actual costs – typically 70–80 per cent. (Some companies apply both limits; it avoids their having to pay for the most expensive schools in the home location.)

Costs are usually limited to the actual fees together with books and other materials, though a few companies pay for school uniforms and ancillary expenses (laundry, essential sports equipment etc). Reunion air fares, in the form of two annual round trips to the assignment country, are normally provided. Occasionally, this is extended to three trips when the employee's annual home leave does not coincide with a school's vacation period.

The problem of having to pay for boarding school on repatriation can be an expensive one. Choosing a school which also takes day pupils and is near your home will eliminate the cost of boarding but fees paid from after-tax income can still be horrendous. A few companies recognize this problem and pay for schooling costs for a limited period on return if a child is at a particularly critical point in his or her education – normally for a period of one to three years. You may have to pay the tax on this benefit.

This argument can be extended to other special cases. Take, for example, the UK national assigned to the USA, or to a country where an American school system was the only option. On returning to the UK, it would not be unreasonable for him to argue that his son or daughter should be able to continue his or her education at one of the American schools near London. Again, the one- to three-year limit would apply.

Post-secondary education

Very few companies pay for university or other tertiary level education. The right to some form of schooling assistance usually ends at the age of 18 or 19 when children are still in full-time education. Some companies provide advice and guidance on university entrance requirements in the employee's home country, but no financial assistance would normally be offered other than perhaps one or two annual, round-trip reunion air fares from the home base to the country of assignment.

Counselling on university entrance requirements is particularly important for UK-based employees and, if your employer is unwilling to offer guidance, it is vital to take professional advice from an education specialist. If stringent residency requirements are not met during the years preceding university entrance, your child will not qualify for the grants which make university education affordable in Britain.

Taxation

Finally, in many countries the provision of assistance towards schooling costs is considered as a taxable benefit in the hands of the employee. You should check whether or not you will be expected to pay this tax – as always, a fundamental issue for those receiving a tax equalized package or one which is stated on purely net terms. In some locations, tax can be legitimately avoided if the school fees are paid directly by the employer or if the company establishes a trust arrangement with a particular school, whereby sums of money are made available to the trust for the benefit of unspecified students. While this can be complicated, it may save you (or your employer for those receiving net packages) significant amounts of money.

18. Medical Care

There is nothing worse than being ill when you are away from home. If you are living, more or less permanently, hundreds or even thousands of miles from the doctors and dentists you have probably visited for years, the potential difficulties can seem even greater. You will wonder about the quality of medical treatment, the problems of trying to communicate in a different language and, above all, how much it is all going to cost.

For these very good reasons, it is extremely important to satisfy yourself that adequate provision for medical care has been made by your employer.

State medical schemes

In many countries, especially in Europe, medical facilities administered by the state are of a perfectly adequate standard and most companies will expect assignees to use them. If this is what you are offered, you will need to know how much, and in what way, you are expected to contribute towards the cost. This will vary enormously, of course, depending on the country. In Britain, for example, contributions to the state social security system, deducted as a percentage of salary, cover the vast majority of costs and only prescription charges and a small number of other items are paid for directly. (Dental charges are also heavily subsidized in this way though you will have to pay up to £150–£200 for more complex forms of treatment.) In France, approximately 70–80 per cent of bills will be reimbursed through a state programme.

While state-operated schemes exist in other parts of the world, the standards are generally quite low and most expatriates would be well advised not to accept employment where they are the only option on offer.

Private medical insurance

Private medicine is a common arrangement for large numbers of expatriates, usually backed by some form of commercially available

BUPA
International Lifeline

Wherever you work or retire, you don't have to go without BUPA.

When it comes to overseas health care, you'll find BUPA goes to the ends of the Earth to help.

insurance to reimburse the majority of costs. Larger organizations tend to operate a single, global plan covering all expatriate staff. In smaller companies, a locally insured plan in the work location is more common.

Cost reimbursement

In terms of who pays for what, it is rare for a company to pay 100 per cent of all medical bills. The typical split is probably somewhere in the region of 75 per cent for the company and 25 per cent for the employee. The cost-sharing arrangements vary considerably. Some are managed as a straightforward company reimbursement of 70–80 per cent of all recognized bills. A deductible programme is also frequently used where the employee pays the first few hundred pounds or dollars of bills each year and the company meets 100 per cent of costs thereafter. A few companies operate on the basis of reimbursing all major medical costs to do with hospitalization and post-operative care but contribute only modestly, if at all, to the expense of 'coughs and colds' visits to a doctor's surgery.

The situation with dental care is not so clear cut. There are many companies who pay nothing towards dental treatment and a few who pay everything. Where companies do pay towards the cost, they will be unlikely to pay for cosmetic dentistry or for treatment that could wait until the employee or family member returns to the home base, either on leave or at the end of the assignment. Payment for eye care, especially for contact lenses, tends not to be reimbursed though there are some exceptions (eg for employees required to work for long periods in front of computer screens).

Not surprisingly, the basis for most policies tends to be the common practice in the country in which the company's headquarters are situated. This accounts, at least in part, for the wide variation in levels of coverage.

Common features of medical plans

- A maximum level of coverage usually applies, either to each type of expense (eg the amount paid towards the daily cost of a hospital bed) or as an absolute upper limit, each year. In globally established plans, this is often a world-wide tariff which can lead to occasional problems if the applicable limit is considerably below the actual costs incurred.
- The plan for expatriates usually covers both the employee and the accompanying family members. Occasionally, the employee will be expected to pay the additional premiums for whole family insurance.

- Coverage for medical treatment tends to continue while the employee is on leave. If the home country has a state medical plan, however, most employers will expect it to be used if the employee or family members are still eligible. You should always check that any insurance provision will continue while on holiday in another country. It may be necessary, for example, to take additional cover when visiting the USA.
- Certain types of medical treatment are frequently excluded on the premiss that, for treatment to be paid for, it must be considered by a qualified doctor to be clinically necessary. This automatically excludes most kinds of cosmetic surgery and may also eliminate what some consider to be 'fringe' medicine such as homoeopathy and acupuncture
- A clause is frequently included stating that the company reserves the right to return the employee to the home location if the period of treatment is likely to be lengthy. This is a reasonable condition; continuing to pay for expatriate costs indefinitely is obviously a burden which any organization will want to avoid.

Where do policies differ?

There are a number of areas of coverage (apart from dental and optical treatment) which are subject to widely differing approaches, and you should check to determine what arrangements are in force for you and your family:

- Maternity benefits are usually covered for the wife of an employee but in some cases this will only extend to surgical costs for a caesarian section or other complications.
- For female employees, the whole question of maternity benefits can be sensitive. While the hospitalization costs for the confinement will often be included as part of the overall level of medical insurance, there is little consensus on the provisions made for maternity leave. Female employees, coming from European countries where state regulations decree long periods of paid and unpaid leave, both before and after the confinement, will understandably expect a similar level of flexibility during an assignment. This is particularly expensive, of course, during expatriation. Since female employees still form only a small fraction of the total expatriate population, many companies have yet to formalize a policy on this issue. If you are likely to be affected, you would be well advised to discuss the probable arrangements with your employer prior to departure. Will you be

expected to return to the home base for the confinement and, if so, at what point? How much time will be allowed for maternity leave and will your position be kept vacant until you return?

• Policies allowing employees some flexibility to be treated in a location other than the one to which they have been assigned also tend to vary, especially when the assignment is in a less well-developed country where they may feel that the medical facilities are inadequate. If you discover, from colleagues working for other companies in your assignment country, that they and their families are sent elsewhere for better quality treatment, it is difficult to accept your employer's view that you should use local hospitals and doctors.

Even when the option to be treated in a country with better facilities is available, you will need to know exactly what you have to pay for and what will be covered by your employer. Apart from the cost of the treatment itself, the most obvious items for discussion will be:

- Travel costs between the two locations, not only for the family member who is unwell but also, for example, for a mother who may need to accompany a sick child.
- Accommodation expenses for accompanying family members. In the case of pregnancy, this may also involve a lengthy period of accommodation cost for the expectant mother since she will probably not be allowed to travel less than one month before the anticipated date of confinement.
- Travel expenses and time off for the employee to visit the family member who is being treated if the period of treatment is prolonged.

Special problems

One other field of medical coverage which is handled with widely differing degrees of sympathy is the general area of rehabilitation. The stresses and strains of expatriate life can sometimes put employees, or members of their families, in a position where they may need psychiatric counselling, specialist help with an alcohol problem or advice on how to reconstruct a failing marriage. In the home base, it would be unusual to turn to an employer for assistance; when overseas, it may be the only alternative.

While many companies may state that their policies specifically exclude this kind of treatment, they are often only too willing to try to help with appropriate contacts and sometimes with financial assistance.

In return, they may ask to be kept informed about how well the treatment is working so that a longer-term plan can be formulated for the employee and the position he is occupying in the work location. Some employees are understandably reluctant to discuss these problems with their employers, fearing that it will damage their career prospects or force a curtailment of the posting. While this is always a risk, it should be borne in mind that the employer often has a great deal invested in making the assignment a success and he will be equally unwilling to let it fail without devoting some effort to finding a workable solution.

Medical examinations

Many companies expect employees and their families to undergo a thorough medical examination before they embark on an overseas posting. This is an obvious and sensible precaution in order to minimize the risk of having to pay for costly treatment and suffer lost working days once the assignment has begun.

There is an increasing trend towards providing these medical checks on a regular basis during the period of expatriation as a form of ongoing preventive maintenance. This is particularly prudent for assignments to less well-developed countries, where illnesses such as tuberculosis still exist and need to be detected at an early stage if they are to be treated quickly and effectively.

Precautions

If you suffer from a medical condition which requires permanent medication (for example, a thyroid deficiency), it is always far more sensible to make this known to your employer at the outset. It will rarely be considered a reason for cancelling the appointment but if you do not mention it, and complications arise during the assignment, there will understandably be less inclination on the part of your employer to help. If you are moving to a remote location, with little access to a reliable supply of sophisticated medicines, you should obviously ship large quantities of whatever you require to avoid any shortfall.

For this kind of assignment, you should also take emergency packs of general medical supplies such as hypodermic needles, sterile pre-packed dressings and even blood plasma. Most doctors will be able to advise on what will be necessary and it is possible to buy standard packs containing all the essential items.

Emergency evacuation

Another sensible precaution for difficult countries, or for employees who travel regularly to remote locations, is to arrange emergency evacuation insurance. This can be obtained from most major insurers (in the UK both BUPA and PPP will be able to help) or directly from organizations which specialize in this kind of service. If, for example, you suffer a heart attack in China, it may be difficult to find a hospital with the kind of facilities you would expect in the West. A phone call to the emergency evacuation service will ensure that you are given the best chance of making a full recovery. They will send a specialist physician, who speaks your language as well as Chinese, to review the type of treatment you are receiving. If he thinks it advisable, you will be transported rapidly to a hospital in Hong Kong, in the care of trained staff, where you will undoubtedly receive much higher standards of medical attention. While one always hopes that this type of situation will not arise, it is extremely comforting to know that such a professional service is available if it does.

Finally, what can you do if, for some reason, your employer is unwilling to provide an adequate medical policy during your assignment? The only option, apart from taking a chance that you will not become ill, will be to find an insurance company willing to set up an individual medical plan for you. Fortunately, there are a number of organizations offering this type of package at reasonable prices. PPP in the UK, for example, have created an individual insurance scheme for expatriates and their families which operates just about anywhere in the world. Premiums vary depending on where the insurance cover will be needed; it will be more expensive, for example, to include the USA. Although you will be expected to pay an initial deductible on most types of treatment, the scheme generally represents good value for money.

19. Wheels and Worthwhile Perks

While perhaps not in the same class as *Lifestyles of the Rich and Famous* the lucky expatriate can acquire a remarkable number of perks that add to his quality of life. This may not be apparent to the expatriate oilfield engineer living in his desert Portacabin but it might cross the mind of a senior executive based in Hong Kong as he is whisked up to his Peak residence by chauffeured BMW, planning the social events of the week and relishing his weekend escape on the company junk.

By definition, this chapter is a pot-pourri of possible perks that you might enjoy as part of the overseas assignment. It is unlikely that any one person would be able to collect all of them, but equally, most expatriates will be on the receiving end of some.

* * *

Picture this scenario: Mr Expat is on a five-year contract with his company in the lovely Asian country of Alaysia. He naturally is a member of the management bonus programme and expects to receive a fair number of stock options each year. As he is an expatriate, he is paid a foreign service premium together with a hardship allowance, although his colleagues have never really understood where exactly the hardship manifests itself. He receives a monthly cost of living allowance on a portion of his salary as imported goods are costly in Alaysia. In practice, his maid, paid by the company, does the shopping at the local market where the food is fresh and the prices reasonable. Mr Expat has a lovely family who live in a company-provided house which has a small swimming pool, bar and BBQ area. While Mrs Expat scours the local markets looking for antiques which she will ship back at the end of the assignment, the junior Expats attend the local international school. The fees are outrageous but fortunately they are picked up by the company. When summer term is finished the whole family disappears for five weeks, first-class return air fares provided.

Mr Expat is taken to work in the chauffeured company car, which sometimes returns to help Mrs Expat undertake shopping trips. At work Mr Expat has a super-efficient office team which makes quite a contrast to the rude bunch of yahoos he worked with back home. The office is one of those air-conditioned towers glittering in the hot Alaysian sun. At lunchtime, he frequently goes to his city club which offers good food and a gym facility in case he is feeling energetic. The club is pleasant but pales in comparison with the golf and country club which the family uses in the evenings and at weekends. If social life at the club gets a bit boring the family can escape in the company boat to the offshore islands, where they say the fishing is always excellent.

Sometimes Mr Expat feels he has been forgotten by headquarters and that his career has been sidetracked. Fortunately, this is partly compensated for by the thought of the end of contract bonus and the enhanced international staff pension plan. If things really foul up in Alaysia, he can always invoke the parachute clause in his contract which gives him five years' salary in event of a parting of the ways.

* * *

A fairy tale perhaps, but one which more fortunate expatriates would recognize and which the company needs to cost into the overseas assignment overheads. Most of Mr Expat's ideal package is discussed in other parts of this book – housing, domestic help, education, pensions, vacations etc – but here we look at two fairly common perks not covered elsewhere: the company car and the club membership.

Company car

The provision of the company car is an emotive issue for expatriate employees as it is for home country-based staff. The company car question overseas, however, raises a number of issues not always apparent in the employee's home country. You will normally be expatriated without your own vehicle (unless you ship it with foreign plates – a procedure which is not recommended) and many companies do provide a car, particularly if prices are high and/or the vehicle difficult to obtain.

Expatriates in developing countries will seldom be prepared to make use of local transport arrangements, assuming that they exist. With the provision of a car comes the issue of who may use it and for what purposes? Some sort of decision has to be taken on whether the wife and other members of the family should be insured, not an easy decision if local driving conditions are particularly difficult. Usually, the expatriate will be able to use the car on days off but should this be extended to allowing him to take the company vehicle on an extended two-week safari?

If the employee drives there is always the possibility of involvement in local accidents, resulting in death or injury. In many countries this can be a sensitive issue as concepts of guilt, punishment and compensation vary a great deal between cultures. The expatriate who kills a local inhabitant in Papua New Guinea would not be well advised to discuss insurance liability with the relatives. Equally, Arab countries often gaol everybody involved in a motor accident, frequently for long periods, while ascertaining what sort of compensation or punishment is considered suitable by the relatives involved.

Some expatriate locations are considered to be so hazardous, in terms of driving conditions, that companies will not allow their expatriate staff to drive vehicles. This was certainly a common feature in many African and Asian countries, particularly where urban driving is considered to be very dangerous. In these cases, the provision of a local driver removes the expatriate from immediate involvement in any ensuing accident. An issue related to this is where, because of local custom, the expatriate's wife is not allowed to drive – Saudia Arabia being the prime example. The company is faced with a choice of either providing a car and driver for the wife (common only for the wives of senior executives) or organizing car pools and children's school buses. The expatriate family, bereft of a car, may soon feel trapped without transport and the resulting low morale will reflect on the expatriate's work performance.

The club

The local club is an institution in many expatriate locations. This may be the local watering hole for the isolated 'colonial' posting or an exclusive golf club membership in Japan, Taiwan or Hong Kong. The appeal is probably the same in both cases – an island of calm and tranquillity away from the work environment where expatriates can mix together. In former times, this may have been at the complete exclusion of the locals, except for the waiter arriving with the gins. Now the mixture is more normally the local élite together with the company-sponsored expatriates. Golf, sailing, tennis, squash or swimming form the main attractions in most of these marble Shangri-Las – to relax the executive and keep the family happy. Anyone new to expatriate employment should realize that what might appear unwelcome paternalism in the home country may be seen as a clear company responsibility in the expatriate community.

One thing to bear in mind about club membership these days is that the cost of membership debentures can often be astronomic. A golf club debenture in Japan or Hong Kong can run into hundreds of thousands of pounds. Even family leisure clubs with a pool and restaurant can be very expensive indeed – the more exclusive, the more expensive. The company may well baulk at this cost when you suggest it. One useful strategy is to demonstrate that buying a company-owned, transferable debenture will prove a great investment, so that in fact you are really doing the company a favour. The smart operator will then buy the membership back from the company at book price when the assignment comes to an end. You should also check who is paying the monthly subscriptions which can be high. Typically, this will be you rather than your employer.

Conclusion

It has become a cliché that the expatriate lives like a king in his overseas location. First, this is not always the case. Few European or North American expatriations will offer much in benefits which are not enjoyed by all executive staff. Second, in some remote locations, the car, the club etc may simply not be available. Even where the expatriate can take advantage of all the benefits, there lies the hidden danger of the green eye syndrome. When the boss visits from head office and sees the huge house, the chauffeured limo and the splendid club, he may feel that you are getting a better deal than he is. That can often mean that the party will soon be over. The wise expatriate, of course, anticipates this situation and turns up to the airport to meet visiting executives in a self-driven battered station wagon. Only the most run-down establishments are used for entertainment and visitors are steered away from the home. In the end, however, the overall cost of providing benefits cannot be hidden and this is the real equation. Will the company be prepared to pay for all the extras to keep you in the location? In the end, that is something which every expatriate must take into account and make his or her own judgement on.

20. Vacations

Vacations – images of hot beaches, swaying palm trees and cool drinks – mean a few weeks away from it all. This may be the popular vision of vacations but for the expatriate it can be the classic case of 'coals to Newcastle' ... sand, palm trees and exotic places may be the very things that he is trying to get away from!

The main issues regarding vacations usually concern duration, a consistent policy and the air ticket. Related issues involve questions of local holidays, field breaks and compassionate leave.

Vacation time

The employer often has strong views about expatriates and their vacations. The vacation is seen as a time to visit home, keep in touch with one's roots and refresh the spirit. Implied in all this is the fear that all expatriates, if left alone in the overseas location, will eventually go a little 'bush' – losing touch with the home culture, correct business practice and perhaps reality altogether. Thus a regular vacation is seen as a valuable antidote to such tendencies.

Linked with this view is the frequent concession that expatriates actually enjoy longer vacations than their domestic counterparts. This is certainly common practice with European companies who will often allow six weeks' vacation for all their expatriates, regardless of seniority – a substantially better deal than the home-based package. American companies, however, have always had a more puritanical attitude towards vacations and this will often be reflected in their expatriate policies. A two- or three-week total allowance time in the States may be extended a few days for travel time but this will be the only concession to the rigours of expatriate life.

For the expatriate, the case for a higher accrual of vacation than he would normally expect at home is clear. Factors involved are the degree of social isolation of the posting, the lower frequency of holiday taken and the length of travel time in returning home. Hardship encountered in a location, although sometimes compensated for financially, should also be rewarded by longer or more vacations.

Equal treatment

A problem arises in formulating a vacation policy where the company employs expatriates of many nationalities. With one nationality the domestic policy can be adapted with a suitable vacation bonus for expatriation. What happens when employees come from many different countries with varied vacation practices? Obviously, American expatriates with three-week domestic vacations will not be impressed when their European counterparts disappear for six weeks! In practice, most international companies come up with some sort of compromise plan which manages to satisfy all their expatriates. A cross-section of vacation entitlements for companies employing expatriates in a number of different locations is shown below.

> *Company A* Europe 3.25 days a month
>   Overseas 4.3 days a month
>   Travel time 1–3 days depending on location
>   Leave taken after 12 months completed

> *Company B* Europe 42 days after 12 months' service
>   Non-Europe 48 days
>   Desert and tropical 54 days
>   Extreme conditions 60 days

> *Company C* W Europe 25 days plus travel
>   E Europe 33 days plus travel
>   Saudi Arabia 44 days plus 8 days' travel

With the cost of transport, and the necessity of establishing a stable expatriate workforce, it is common practice to limit vacation periods to once or twice a year and only after the expatriate has completed one year of expatriation. In these days of air travel, this is a world away from the expatriate regime of leave once every five years with the first-class cabin in the luxurious ocean liner. The memory of those days still lingers on, however, with the trip home being a high point of the year.

The vacation air ticket

Some issues seem small matters on the surface but never fail to generate a lot of heat – the use of the annual vacation air ticket is one of these 'hot potatoes'.

Because many companies see the annual vacation as an essential pilgrimage to the home country, they often set restrictions on the use of your holiday air ticket. The employment contract will usually state that the company will pay for a return ticket to the point of origin for the family on a once-a-year basis. Depending on the generosity of the policy this will either be economy, business or first class. So far, so good. The problems arise when you, say based in Saudi Arabia, wish to take your family off to Kenya on safari instead of returning to Europe. Will the company give you the cash equivalent of the tickets or pay for the alternative travel arrangements or perhaps refuse to pay anything at all? This sort of situation never fails to raise the expatriate's anger – clearly the company would have spent the money anyway so should give you the full cash amount. Not so fast, argues the personnel department. Giving the cash provides a substantial windfall for someone who lives a long way from the assignment and discriminates against the individual who lives relatively close by.

Some companies take a hard line and only provide actual tickets to the point of origin; others are happy to hand over the cash, despite the potential problems. A middle course is to pay for air tickets up to the price of the original ticket but not to cover any other types of expense. In this case the expatriate would get his flights paid from Saudi to Kenya but any surplus in the price of the tickets would not be handed over to pay for hotel accommodation.

Local holidays

Clearly, local holidays given in different countries round the world vary considerably – both as to when they occur and their frequency. For the cunning expatriate, countries like Nepal with 30 days of public holiday a year offer a good deal whereas Saudi Arabia (one public holiday) and Pakistan (seven public holidays) look like poor prospects. Most companies will, however, accept that the frequency of local holidays is just one of the vagaries of operating internationally and will not attempt to legislate whether it is legitimate or not for the expatriate to take these days off. This is anyway a matter of practicality, given that there will be no local staff around during any holiday period.

* * *

A slightly more complicated variation is the expatriate who insists on marking his own country's holidays. The Jewish American based in France may end up taking off Yom Kippur as well as the 4th of July and Bastille Day. It may sound extreme but does occur from time to time.

* * *

Field breaks

The field break, sometimes known as hardship leave or rest and recreation, is something of an institution in a few of the tougher expatriate locations. The theory is that, in places where conditions are rough, the expatriate should be allowed to take several short breaks during the year in addition to his regular vacation. These breaks will usually be to locations nearby that contrast with the place of assignment. Some companies will formulate a separate policy on field breaks for single staff, following the logic that singles need the break more as they lack the company of a spouse.

A typical field break policy looks something like this:

Field breaks are granted to permanent expatriates in the following locations ...

Two field breaks of five days are allowed to married couples and three breaks of five days to single-status staff on an annual basis.

An economy air ticket is provided to the nearest point of interest selected by the regional manager. Hotel fees will be paid.

There is no change of salary during the field break and this leave does not affect vacation entitlement.

Field breaks do not accrue if not taken and cannot be pooled with the annual vacation.

Equipped with this policy, the company hopes that its expatriates will return to their desert, jungle or urban jungle locations refreshed and invigorated, ready to face the frustrations of their particular assignment. They will also be able to replenish stocks of food, toiletries, medical supplies etc unavailable in the work location.

Compassionate or emergency leave

By moving a family sometimes thousands of miles away from relations and friends, the employer takes on a moral responsibility that would not exist in the domestic environment. Deaths in the family, problems with children left at home or simply domestic business matters can force a rapid return of the expatriate to the home base even if it is only for a matter of a few days. Most companies accept this and will give the time off, either as part of the vacation allowance or as additional leave. A more difficult decision is who pays for the air fare, and here companies seem evenly split between offering to pay and insisting that it is the responsibility of the expatriate and his family.

Accommodation during vacation

A family of four, returning to the home base for a few weeks, will be faced with the headache of where to stay and how to travel around to visit all their relatives. Most companies will say it's your problem and you will often find yourself saddled with a huge bill at the end of the holiday for car rental and short-term house rental. (Staying with members of your family is OK for a short period but, as the Germans say, after a few days the fish start to smell ...)

One solution is to pay a small subscription to a house-swapping organization. The details of your property are entered in a biannual publication with hundreds of others and you then make direct contact with those contributors whose properties meet your particular needs. When you find the ideal match, you simply arrange to live in each other's houses for the agreed period. One of the hidden advantages of expatriation is that you often have an attractive home in your work location which many other people would love to live in (and help to keep secure) while you are away. In return, you can live in their house, rent free, often with a car thrown into the deal. You should, of course, check that this will not be a problem with your employer and the company insuring the house and contents. One useful contact in the UK is Interhouse, which specializes in vacation house swapping.

Expatriates used to travel POSH – port out and starboard home – on their journeys to India and the Far East (the shadier side of the ship). Now they pack the innards of 747s, particularly around the months of July and August. They will usually, as in the past, be travelling home to catch up with relatives and friends. The world may have become a smaller place but vacations are still one of the highlights of the expatriate year – to be looked forward to, discussed on return and, with luck, actually enjoyed when being taken.

21. Domestic Staff

Westerners visiting South America or Asia on business often feel uneasy in the presence of servants when invited to the homes of their local counterparts. And yet, as expatriates resident in these locations, employing domestic help soon becomes a normal and sensible practice.

Using low-cost local or imported labour to perform the mundane tasks of life has its supporters and critics. The fact of the matter is that, in Asia, Africa and South America, it is perfectly natural for any reasonably affluent family to employ servants and, moreover, it is viewed as a service to the country. There is little point in being over-sensitive about what is seen as one of the most significant pluses of expatriation, even though it may be viewed with general distaste in the egalitarian West.

Even in London and New York, au pairs, nannies and gardeners are seen as essential to the well-being of busy middle-class families with executive lifestyles. There is, however, a world of difference between Heidi in Kensington, who keeps an eye on the children for a few hours each day before borrowing the family car to visit her friends, and Conchita in Singapore, who works 70 hours a week and has to wash the family car.

Having exposed the moral dilemma, it should be laid to rest quickly in order to review the practicalities of hiring and keeping domestic help. Those with strong feelings about what they see as unacceptably repressive should read no further; for those who want the easy life (and those who secretly envy it), read on.

Availability

In many parts of Asia and the Middle East, domestic staff come from the Philippines or Sri Lanka. This is less the case in some countries, such as India and Indonesia, where locals can be hired with little difficulty. In Africa and South America, domestic help is usually from the poorer section of the local population. While staff are usually female, they may be houseboys. In some countries, where local labour is extremely cheap, it is quite common to take on several members of the same family, in a packaged deal, providing cook, house cleaner, gardener, driver etc. (This is frequently the case in the Indian sub-continent and Africa.)

Recruitment sources vary enormously. In Singapore and the Middle East, for example, agencies exist specifically for the purpose of procuring hired help from other countries. For a fee, the agency will handle the entire process of identifying a suitable candidate, securing the necessary employment papers and making travel arrangements. For a Westerner, it can be a depressing experience to sit in a fly-blown office in Abu Dhabi flicking through a catalogue of poor quality photographs and reading the mini-biographies of hopeful contenders. But often the process is more humane. Much is done by word of mouth and 'Wanted' ads on supermarket noticeboards.

Having made contact, the process of interviewing can be quite a challenge. There is an obvious need to be able to communicate reasonably clearly to avoid misunderstandings. If an applicant has had no experience with a western family and only looked after a couple with school-aged children, she will probably find it difficult to cope with an American family with three infants under five. It is surprising how such basic mismatching problems are often overlooked in the initial stages of discussion.

❋ ❋ ❋

The following is a classic piece of misunderstanding which arose with a maid fresh from a remote village on Mindanao. On being asked to 'put some lemon in the gin and tonic' for a guest, she presented a drink with the whole fruit stuffed in the glass, apologizing that she could not find a lemon small enough to go all the way to the bottom. This should not be seen as a joke against the maid, but rather as a reflection on the many communication gaps, both linguistic and cultural, often encountered. The 'sophisticated' expatriate should be able to anticipate such cultural chasms. Sadly, all too often such situations are used merely as dinner party anecdotes.

❋ ❋ ❋

The preliminary discussion must, of course, include a clear indication of the duties to be undertaken. A written job description, detailing the various tasks, and when they should be performed, is not an over-bureaucratic precaution, assuming that the prospective candidate is able to read the language of their employer – otherwise it should be translated. The burden to be imposed, in most less well-developed countries, is more a function of the employer's conscience than mandatory official working hours. This may seem cynical but should be seen in the context of the preference of most domestic staff for employment with expatriate/western families who often (but not always) treat them better than local employers. As with any workforce, when there is more than one employee (eg a cook and a maid), it is essential to make a clear distinction as to who does what.

Contracts

In most countries, there is some form of written contract, detailing the terms of employment. Where this is not a legal requirement, it is still prudent to draw up some form of agreement specifying such issues as pay and when it is reviewed, days off, leave, transport to the city of origin etc. Of particular concern should be the arrangements for medical coverage and what will happen, for example, if a domestic helper should become pregnant. Singapore has all these arrangements extremely well planned. Apart from signing a detailed employment contract, the employer is required to buy a government bond, costing several thousand Singaporean dollars, which ensures that a wide variety of potentially expensive crises will be underwritten by the employer (presumably rather than the state).

For those still undeterred by the problems of communication and red tape, there are plenty of other difficulties with which to contend. How much does one pay? (Avoid paying over the odds if maintaining good relations with neighbours is a high priority.) Does this include food and daily needs? (These are often covered by a separate payment but staff may still help themselves to bits and pieces from the fridge, toothpaste, washing powder.) What kind of furniture should be provided for their accommodation? What degree of freedom should be given to leave the home in off-duty hours? There are obviously no global reference points for this kind of thing and the only way to find out is to ask. Local personnel department staff and colleagues are obvious sources of information.

Domestic staff and the local community

In deciding whether or not to hire domestic help (particularly of the permanent, live-in variety), there are a number of additional points to consider.

Experienced local staff know their way around in the local community and, even if they load the bills when they shop on their employer's behalf, this can still be cheaper than buying in stores geared to the local expatriate population.

* * *

In Jakarta, domestic staff are an important link with the 'village chief' who has unwritten authority over the particular district in which the expatriate lives. The city operates with various levels of civic administration and it is important not to dismiss this individual as a relic of some primitive rural past. He can, for example, help to recover stolen goods but, if ignored, may be inclined to arrange for car wrecks to be dumped in the drive-way of a foreigner's home.

* * *

Although servants normally live in a separate part of a house or apartment, they are a part of it and this can be intrusive for people who like to do as they please. It becomes difficult, for example, to wander around clad only in yesterday's underwear when the maid is trying to vacuum the lounge carpet.

Following on from this theme is the sensitive issue of just how far conventions allow the maid to become 'a part of the family'. In an effort to salvage their collective conscience on the moral issue of hiring cheap labour to perform menial tasks, some families try to include their domestic helper as a kind of adopted son or daughter, insisting that they eat together and that the maid shares in the social life of the household. This is well meant but can bring disastrous results; domestic staff are often embarrassed by the proximity and would prefer to spend their time with friends who understand them. Most would be satisfied with maintaining a distant respect rather than be forced into aping behaviour and attitudes which they find, for the most part, incomprehensible.

Living with someone whose vision of the world has been based on the back streets of Manila or a jungle village outside São Paolo can sometimes be frustrating. Moral values are often quite different from those in the West – and often not in the sense of being lower. There are, of course, maids who take evenings off to supplement their incomes by working at the oldest profession in the world when the fleet is in; others spend all their free time studying the Bible. Some manage to do both. This requires an adjustment in attitude, on the part of the employer, which is not always easy to accomplish.

* * *

Some moral questions are harder to answer than others. A maid in Hong Kong, when asked by a prospective employer what her previous people had paid her, replied '$3400 per month and $50 each time ma'am had a headache'.

* * *

There is a belief that employers are sometimes willing to pay for domestic servants. This can be a useful benefit but, apart from some very senior staff, and in those situations where the employee must entertain frequently at home in difficult surroundings, it is not a commonly provided extra. Most companies take the view that it is not their responsibility to run the employee's household and do not want to over-involve themselves in the time-consuming and often acrimonious problems that can arise. One exception would be providing a driver in countries where the difficulties of parking and moving around the city on business are such that a chauffeur is essential for efficiency. Caracas and Bangkok are good examples of this.

A final piece of advice: it is essential to have a good sense of humour to be able to take the multitude of minor daily crises in your stride. It also helps to learn a few words of the language in which the domestic helper is most comfortable. A knowledge of Tagalog or Tamil may not be of much use beyond the immediate future but it can pay enormous dividends in maintaining a little sanity during an assignment.

22. Financial Advice

Introduction

To many expatriates, the very definition of a good assignment is a matter of how much surplus income can be accumulated for the duration of the overseas stay. Employers may, of course, consider this attitude lamentable – stressing that there are other things to consider such as career development, cultural enrichment, and the opportunity to cultivate tolerance and racial harmony. The reality is usually that the main lure of an expatriate assignment will be the ability to save a far greater proportion of salary than was ever possible at home.

The equation on savings is not a simple one and certainly not a matter of merely measuring the level of salary. The main benefit of expatriation is that the salary is frequently not exposed to the overheads of living at home. First and foremost come tax arrangements where the expatriate can certainly hope for (even if not always obtain) a more generous tax regime – even to the extent of pay net of tax or, alternatively, the zero tax regimes of the Middle East. Second on the list of financial burdens is usually housing, whereby paying rent or servicing the mortgage will take away a sizeable percentage of disposable income. Again, the expatriate can often enjoy a break by living in free or subsidized housing overseas and by renting out his property at home while he is away.

There may, of course, be other breaks in the expatriate package which reduce financial overheads – paid education for the children, company car, 100 per cent health cover and a generous expense allowance which would raise more than a few eyebrows if allowed on home turf. Lastly, the foreign service premium and cost of living allowance (COLA) of the package can often be banked in hard cash rather than spent on buying expensive imported brand names. An expatriate family who adjust to the local market can shop as cheaply as everyone else, thus making the elaborate COLA arrangement somewhat superfluous.

All these add up to surplus cash, probably more than will ever be available to an executive at other times in his or her career. And where cash accumulates, financial advice and advisers abound – a mini-industry living, some would say parasitically, on the good fortune of the expatriate.

Let us take a typical situation. Mr Jones has a three-year contract in Hong Kong which pays US$100,000 a year with free housing, 15 per cent local tax and an expectation of a 20 per cent bonus a year. On top of this, he receives a cost of living allowance that pays US$700 a month. Being realistic, he thinks he can save perhaps $6000 a month – or with luck nearly $250,000 for the duration of his assignment.

Offshore havens

The first thing an expatriate will want to know is how he can build up this $250,000 without incurring tax on the interest or capital gains derived from investing the capital. Bobbing away just over the horizon are the famous (or perhaps infamous) offshore tax havens – Guernsey, Jersey, the Cayman Islands, Bermuda, Luxembourg, Gibraltar, even the Cook Islands spring to mind. These exotic locations all encourage the expatriate to park his money with them with little or no government interference on boring matters like tax. This has resulted in a cottage industry of brass plate makers establishing legal entities for banks, offshore funds and the like which serve as vehicles for expatriate cash.

Advisers

A normal experience for any expatriate two or three months into his assignment is the friendly phone call from the local financial adviser. These people come in all shapes and forms: some are based in the home country and travel; others cover an area of overseas territory. They tend to accumulate prospective clients by networking around the expatriate community – the clubs, golf clubs and watering holes patronized as a home away from home. A new expatriate in town will always provide an opportunity to see if any new business can be generated. The rule with a financial adviser is to remember that he is anything other than disinterested, however professionally he presents his recommendations. Advisers derive their income from commissions, retainers and bonuses based on amounts of money that they direct into the financial institutions, and usually the more exotic the investment, the higher the commission received by the financial adviser.

Although advisers range through the spectrum of bank manager to unsolicited but free advice from a barfly you chance to drink next to, there are a few distinct categories:

Independent financial adviser (IFA)

The genuine IFA is a valuable contact. The title infers that his (or her) investment advice is entirely based on judgement concerning the investors' needs and past performance of the investment funds. This may not always be true as the most independent of IFAs may have particular favourites and be influenced by attractive commission rates.

Product affiliated

It may not always be apparent but many investment advisers are in fact tied to one organization and one range of products. The most common example is the insurance salesman who can now dress himself in all sorts of camouflage but at the end of the day is still selling you a life insurance policy. Some organizations sell their own products together with a range of others, although one would have to suspect that the final investment decision might be biased in favour of the mother company.

Payment by results

A number of the smaller investment concerns will build up an entirely independent portfolio but link payments to the results obtained. With the good ones, this can be well worth the money; for example, 50 per cent of the profits above a 20 per cent annual return. The danger to watch for is the fine print: exactly what is the payment formula and how risky are the investments in the gamble for success? After all, no company volunteers to share in your losses.

Fly by night/Boiler shops

Every industry has its share of con merchants and rip-off operators – and, given the low entry costs and potential profits, investment attracts rogues as a jam pot does wasps. There are some warning bells you should not ignore when approached by the fly-by-night investment adviser:

- His claims for profit are often exaggerated – he plays on your greed.
- You will never have heard of the companies that he represents – they will invariably be based in countries lacking stringent investment regulations.
- The investment will often involve a complicated chain where none of the links is easy to check.
- If share purchase is involved, the notorious Vancouver stock market may be tied into the transaction.

With all advisers, the key is to decide your own objectives and stick to them. Never be afraid – even if it means being rude – to resist a sales patter that steers you in a direction that you don't want to travel.

Portfolio spread

Expatriates are no different from any other punters when it comes to investment decisions – a bet on a horse, gold bars or keeping money under the mattress may all be better or worse ways of building a nest egg. However, the only tried and tested rule is to aim for a portfolio spread of various investments with varying degrees of risk. Of course, everything (including doing nothing) involves risk of some sort with inflation eroding all capital over time and all delay involving some sort of opportunity cost.

The portfolio spread should be determined by the proportion invested against the degree of risk. Roughly, in ascending order, risk can go something like this:

Cash (current account/building society)	Safe if the financial institution is safe but currency exposure and low interest may not compensate for inflation.
Money fund	Allows experts to choose balance of various currencies and obtain best interest rates. The danger is that the experts can be wrong! A variant of this is leveraged money funds that scale up the risk and reward.
Bonds	Bonds and bond funds range from the junk variety to government gilts. Used to be boringly safe but can now be surprisingly volatile. Always a juggle between interest rate offered and price.
Blue chip shares	Any spread of a dozen blue chip shares should track the market fairly closely – for better or worse. The expatriate usually dabbles in his home market stock exchange plus the local market where he is posted.
2nd and 3rd liners	As above, but considerably more risky. These are shares of small, infrequently traded companies and carry considerably more risk than the blue chip shares.
Offshore funds	In the last ten years there has been an explosion in offshore funds covering every investment market with a total spectrum of risk. Funds offer a better spread in any given market but their

administration costs can be high and they are only as good as the skill or luck of the current fund manager.

Property

Often the favourite strategy of the expatriate – buy another house back home or in a summer/ski resort. Buying in the country of assignment can be tricky and meet with company disapproval. The only problem with property is that it tends to be illiquid just when you need the cash – and requires constant attention which can be a nuisance.

Exotics

Whether it's commodity futures warrants, being a name at Lloyd's, buying fine art, vintage wines or collecting Ferraris – these are all volatile markets requiring a degree of expertise. The name of the game is high risk/high return.

Looking at the eight categories described above, portfolio spread implies deciding what percentage of your money you want in each area. The investment adviser can help in analysing your cash flow requirements, tax implications, and how actually to go about making the investment. Only you, having acquired the surplus cash, can decide what risk you want to take with it.

Tax

The long-term tax consequences of any financial investment strategy will often make the difference between a mediocre return and a very attractive one. The opportunity to place money in a variety of offshore funds, coupled with your temporary absence from the tax net of the home country, can be used to tremendous effect in building up substantial, long-term, tax-free gains well after the assignment has ended and you are back in your country of origin.

This is particularly relevant for UK-based employees. Current legislation allows you to enter ten-year, insurance-linked, offshore savings plans to which you may continue to contribute after repatriation. If carefully arranged, the capital and interest accumulated in these schemes can be realized with virtually no tax liability arising – often a useful way of saving towards future requirements for large amounts of cash such as school fees. Shorter-term savings schemes, and the purchase of an insurance-linked bond immediately before the return to the home base, can also be extremely tax efficient. Although complicated, it is often beneficial for the individual with substantial assets to establish an offshore trust fund, while overseas, to avoid punitive income and capital gains taxes on return.

Never commit yourself to any investment without knowing what the tax consequences will be, both in the work location and on return to the home base.

23. Insurance and Social Security

There are two things to worry about;
Either you are well or you are sick.
If you are well, then there is nothing to worry about.
But if you are sick,
There are two things to worry about;
Either you will get well or you will die.
If you get well, there is nothing to worry about.
If you die,
There are two things to worry about;
Either you will go to heaven or you will go to hell.
If you go to heaven, there is nothing to worry about.
But if you go to hell,
You'll be so busy shaking hands with friends
You won't have time to worry.

This sensible advice on coping with life and death introduces one of the more tedious aspects of expatriation. If you are anticipating the challenge and adventure of a posting to another country, the last thing you want to deal with is the prospect of dying or becoming permanently disabled.

Nevertheless, it is an important issue and dealt with it must be. Many personnel departments have somebody who specializes in this field so this chapter is a simple review for the benefit of those who require only a quick run-down on the essentials.

Key questions to raise

- If I die, how much cash will my survivors receive in addition to any widow's/orphan's pension?
- If I can't work any more, because of some form of disability, how much do I get and for how long?

- Are these benefits going to be subject to any form of taxation and, if so, can I avoid it?
- Do I contribute in any way towards the cost of their provision in the form of mandatory or voluntary contributions to social security schemes or through a salary deduction of some kind?

Since health insurance is covered elsewhere, this is about the size of the problem unless you are concerned about unemployment benefits (and you ought to be, but thinking about death and disability is bad enough, at the beginning of an assignment, without dwelling on the prospect of losing the job before it even begins).

These questions are more or less the ones you should ask wherever you work. At home or abroad, the problems are not too different; the solutions, however, vary enormously.

The available options

The following chart breaks down the various permutations of coverage which fall under the three main (and progressively life-threatening) headings of *Salary continuation*, *Disability* and *Death*:

An analysis of the options for insurance cover

IS THE RISK COVERED? (SALARY DURING ILLNESS/DISABILITY/DEATH)			
Paid for by insurance?	Company provided?	Home base cover?	Employee contribution required?
	State provided?	Host base cover?	
	Combination?		
Premiums? taxable	Tax deductable to company?	Employee pays tax?	
	Taxable for employee?	Company pays tax?	
Amount varies depending on ...		Occupational cause?	
		Non-occupational cause?	

BENEFITS	
SALARY CONTINUATION DURING ILLNESS	– Duration at full pay? – What pay? (Location or home base?) – Is repatriation required? – Does disability insurance take over?

DEATH	– Lump sum or annuity?
	– If lump sum, variable owing to:
	  • Number of dependants?
	  • Accident or illness?
	  • If accident: Occupational?/Other?
	– What pay basis? (Location or home base?)

DISABILITY	PERMANENT? – Partial or total? (Proportional payment for partial disability) – Duration of payment? – Integration with pension? – What happens on death? – Waiting period for payment? – Lump sum or annuity? (see DEATH above)
	TEMPORARY? – Duration of payment? – Maximum period? – Lump sum or annuity? (see DEATH above) – What pay basis? (Location or home base?)

Understanding these options, and being prepared to ask questions about them, should be enough for most detail-minded (or bloody-minded) employees who want to be fully briefed on every eventuality.

The employee's point of reference

The above chart shows that there are many variables on the extent to which cover might be available. Your interest in the potential value of what you are being offered will be geared to the following factors:

- Your family status.
- Your age (usually a greater concern for those in their 30s and 40s preoccupied with a young family).
- The extent to which pension and insurance schemes in which you continue to participate provide adequate 'death in service/early retirement owing to ill health' features.

- What you are used to in your home base. (Very high lump sum multiples of annual salary are provided in France; the Netherlands has a wide range of generous benefits for those unable to work – financed largely through state programmes.)
- Your perception of the risks involved in the job. This may be an important factor for those involved, for example, in dangerous construction or oil platform work and those who fly frequently on business.

Typical benefits

The extent of coverage can be driven by global as well as local policies. Some companies, for example, operate a 24-hour accidental death and disability policy which applies to all their employees on a blanket coverage basis.

It is difficult to establish an expatriate norm because of the number of variables involved. The following represents a selection of typical benefits which might be available:

- A salary continuation policy providing 100 per cent of salary for 26 weeks followed by a further 26 weeks at 50 per cent of salary. This could also require the employee to repatriate and receive a home base salary once the illness/recovery period is known to be long term.
- An accidental death and disability benefit equivalent to four times the annual salary of the employee. A home base reference salary would normally be used for calculation purposes. The disability policy would have a reduced benefit for partial disability (eg loss of sight; loss of limbs) where the employee is able to find other gainful employment. This would be payable in addition to any general life insurance cover provided by the employer and may be limited to occupational accidents.
- A death benefit/life insurance component, which is often part of the pension arrangement, of one to four times annual salary.

In many cases, this would equate to the typical home base arrangements of a US or other western country-based company. As mentioned above, however, a French or Dutch company may be much more generous (with lump-sum multiples of up to 10 to 12 times annual salary for death resulting from occupational causes and several children surviving the employee; pension payments tend to be correspondingly smaller).

Social security programmes

Whether benefits are derived from local or global plans (and the latter tend to be dominant in organizations with a large, mobile international workforce), the major difficulties arise, for both employer and employee, in marrying company-provided benefits with mandatory state provisions in the country of assignment, particularly in European countries where social benefit programmes are sophisticated.

There is no typical approach to the problem of integrating state and company benefit plans. Some companies completely ignore the provisions of state sickness insurance and workers' compensation programmes, often paying expensive contributions and allowing possible benefits to be claimed by the employee on top of the company plan entitlements; others prefer to analyse the benefits available and build a broadly integrated state and company plan arrangement which meets minimum global standards. For transfers to local operations of companies in European countries, the arrangements made for local staff are often used, especially where transfers are made between European Community countries in which entitlement to full state scheme benefits will often be available without the need to fulfil a minimum contribution period because of the reciprocal arrangements within the EC.

Whichever approach is taken, there are two important points:

- Make sure that you are clear what the deal will be (not only in terms of benefits available during the assignment but also the potential loss of rights which might arise because of your absence from, and lack of contributions to, home-based programmes).
- Check whether or not you are required to make any contributions and, in the case of net or tax-equalized packages, if you are going to be unpleasantly surprised at a reduction in the stated pay level.

As a postscript, here is a contentious point on insurance and expatriation. Should you receive more benefit than your locally employed counterpart simply because you are an expatriate?

Logically, the answer is no. The argument that an expatriate is possibly taking more risks and should therefore receive more benefit is not necessarily true; nor is the argument, in itself, valid that the greater the risk, the greater the reward. Death or disability exacts the same toll and has the same financial and emotional effect on dependants, however great the risk that they might actually arise. In the final analysis, the value of reliable, comprehensive coverage is probably a more significant consideration during expatriation than it is when you are working at home. This is particularly true, for example, if home-based personal insurance cover is not valid while living overseas. Existing insurance policies should therefore be checked as part of the standard preparation for any expatriate assignment.

24. Homeward Bound

And then one day it's all over. The heat of the desert, the smell of the jungle are just memories. The average expatriate assignment lasts for about three years and so, for many families, just as they've settled in, they are on their way back to their home base. On reflection that is the nature of the expatriate job – it is, or at least should be, transitory. After all, an expatriate is only sent to a location because the company feels that this is the best solution, despite the usual cost penalties incurred. You will always be living on borrowed time because there are so many factors that can bring the assignment to an end.

For many companies the motivation to send someone overseas is development – of the subsidiary company or the individual. Either way there comes a point when head office judges that the objective has been achieved. In the rare, well-planned corporate environment, this means that the next job has been arranged and is waiting to be filled. More usually there is a general feeling that it is about time the individual returned from foreign parts. The hidden agenda may be that the time is ripe for localization, with all the cost savings such a change may achieve. Some companies have a policy to move people on every three or four years to avoid the roots growing too deep – 'going bush' with all the nightmares that implies for the management back at HQ. Either way, what lies behind the relocation is less important than the fact that it happens, and for you it means a major upheaval.

On the other hand, the pressure to return home often comes from the expatriate himself or his family. Foreign locations and jobs do not always live up to expectations. There may be health problems or domestic crises that necessitate a move back to the home base.

Clearing up

As Shakespeare wrote, 'If it were done ... then 'twere well it were done quickly.' There is nothing worse than protracted goodbyes and the lame duck syndrome when everyone knows you are on your way. Packing up in a foreign location is usually much easier than making the move overseas from home. If the house is rented and the car company property the difficult problems are already someone else's responsibility. In most locations with an expatriate community, there is a network for selling off surplus furniture and appliances. When the small ad goes up on the office noticeboard, in the local supermarket or on marketline local radio, the vultures quickly gather. Stoves, settees and stereos go for rock-bottom prices and are quickly hauled away.

A more delicate issue is deciding what to keep and then ensuring that it is all packed safely away for the journey home. The elephant table or the Indonesian batik that looked so good in the apartment may not fit in quite so well back in the semi-detached in Surbiton. Some expatriates are so loath to part with all their purchases that the shipment requires a full container.

This can be a tricky point in terms of who pays for what. Invariably, you will leave with more than you brought and some employers are not particularly keen to pay the extra for this. A few companies have policies which provide increasingly high volumes of shipment allowance depending on the length of time away from the home base; others allow you to ship home extra items at the time of home leave. However, this is by no means standard and you should think carefully about the cost of transportation before you make the decision to buy a rosewood dining room suite or a collection of valuable Korean chests.

Once the shipment quotes have been approved, the team of removers arrives and within hours the accumulation of the last three or four years is wrapped, packed and hauled away, leaving a bare, unfamiliar apartment.

Goodbye parties are, of course, one of the common features of expatriate life, given that people are moving on all the time. Usually, they come in threes or fours – one in the office, one at home, possibly one at the club, and another at the home of a best friend with whom you swear frequent and lasting contact. Emotions run high and all those aspects about the place you found irritating suddenly become quaint, cute or romantic. Human nature being what it is, the bad is forgotten and the good idealized. So finally you and your family are at the airport – through the difficult customs controls one more time and on to the plane heading home.

Reverse culture shock

We talk about culture shock when first working overseas, but perhaps the real culture shock happens when we return home. Take Mr Smith who has been working in Africa for the last four years. He and his family did not much like the location when they first arrived. The weather was always hot, the food tasted strange, and the office was pretty much of a shambles. Over the months, however, Mr Smith became accustomed to local ways and rather enjoyed being, for the first time in his career, the unquestioned boss of the patch. Equally, the family, after the initial moans, settled in rather well. Mrs Smith got to know all the other women in the small expat community and built up a lively social life centring on the local yacht and golf clubs. This lifestyle was made easier by the availability of cheap and plentiful domestic help so that, after some initial misunderstandings, the home arrangements ran like clockwork. The two kids took to the local international school right away, made some good friends and seemed to do better academically than at the local comprehensive in England.

Now the Smith family are back at their suburban house in London. The house, which was rented by two tenants during their stay abroad, looks markedly worse for wear and Mr Smith thinks that redecoration will cost at least £5000. The kids are miserable, having left their friends behind in Africa, and are not taking at all well to the rigours of the local school. Mrs Smith finds her days a bit empty as she cannot get back to the job she gave up four years ago and discovers she knows hardly anyone in her old neighbourhood. For Mr Smith the problem is even worse as he has been given a boring desk-bound job at head office. No one wants to hear about his experiences in the overseas branch and he detests the hour-long journey to and from work. He really misses Sam, the driver, and the air-conditioned car. And, of course, all the family just hate the British weather – the cold grey damp of their first winter back home.

Perhaps this is an extreme picture, but many expatriates will recognize aspects of it from their own experiences after a spell overseas. Usually, of course, the feeling of alienation from the home environment quickly wears off but for some it has a lasting effect. This can lead to a desperation to return overseas or a persistent state of depression brought on by feelings about the home base location – the worst type of reverse culture shock. What do you do if you and your family find yourselves in this situation? There are a few solutions. One is straightforward. Get yourself and your family back into the home environment as quickly as possible. For the jobholder this may be relatively easy, provided the new job is interesting and work colleagues not too intolerable. For the family it may be a little more difficult, but new friends and activities do dim the memories of more exotic locations. Another alternative may be more difficult to arrange and could require a change of employer, but for the 'expatriate junkie' it may be the only way to go. Given enough time and determination, most people can arrange another assignment overseas, either by pestering their own company or finding another employer seeking the overseas experience that the returned expatriate can now prove he possesses.

If you find it difficult launching yourself into a new domestic life, and moving abroad again is not practical, there is no real therapy for your problem. Your only option is to seek out other ex-expatriates with similar difficulties and reminisce about the good old days. Your home base friends, who are not particularly interested in your anecdotes about life in the Middle East anyway, certainly will not be sympathetic. In the UK, there has in fact been a tendency for expatriates to congregate in the same parts of the country on their return. While this is partly because of the proliferation of boarding schools taking children with parents overseas, it is no coincidence that the areas around towns like Woking and Guildford in Surrey are considered as desirable places to settle.

Returning salary and benefits

On a more mundane level, a returning expatriate needs to consider what his employer is offering in terms of salary and benefits. If you have been overseas on a short contract tied into a balance sheet, the problem is not necessarily complicated. You will have been given a reference salary while you were away and, all things being equal, that will be the salary on which you return. Moreover, stays overseas of a year or two usually mean that you can retain the home-based benefit system, so that pension and insurance arrangements remain undisturbed. With that in mind, it is usually only a matter of getting used to the pain of the domestic tax regime and the immediate costs of settling down in the home environment. Many companies will provide an allowance for this – perhaps a month of extra salary or something similar.

If the expatriate has been away for some time, the situation may be very different. The salary level overseas may bear no relation to the domestic structure and, without a balance sheet, costing for tax and housing may not have any linkage to the overall package. In this situation, reintegration could be difficult. Imagine that you have been away for ten years with housing provided and no tax liability – not such an unusual state of affairs for many expatriates. Given normal inflation in the home country, it may be virtually impossible for the company to provide a net salary that comes anywhere near the overseas remuneration. The returning expatriate is faced with a substantial drop in income. This is compounded by the inability to measure whether the loss is in base salary, allowances and incentives, or as a result of tax treatment.

The company may go one of three ways when faced with this sort of problem. It may offer nothing, insisting on immediate integration into the local structure. This means that the expatriate has to accept the pain or find another employer. Alternatively, the company may recognize that the longer-term expatriate should be given some lump sum when returning to his home country at the time of repatriation (or even before to make the payment tax effective). If mobility is at a premium, and the employee is only expected to be back in the home base for a few years, a third alternative might be to negotiate a front- and back-end payment:

Pre-transfer bonus (paid overseas before repatriation) – four months' salary
Post-transfer bonus (paid overseas after leaving home country) – four months' salary.

If you are faced with returning to your home base after a long spell overseas, it is well worth suggesting this type of approach to buffer yourself against the almost inevitable loss of net income.

Benefits accrued overseas

Social security programmes are dealt with in more detail in Chapters 13 and 23. The key point for a returning expatriate is to remember that, after a number of years, his or her contribution to overseas social security programmes may result in worthwhile long-term benefits. Anyone living in France, for example, has to pay into the national scheme and the inflation-linked 'points' provide a pension income when the time comes. This or similar approaches apply in a number of countries. On the other hand, some local plans may well be worthless the minute the plane door closes. Either way, the home-based company may not have taken any of this into account in the administration of its own pension planning. The expatriate must therefore push for an overall retirement umbrella to ensure reasonable benefit levels and reintegration into the home country plan.

Education of children

The problems which arise with schooling arrangements on return to the home base are covered in Chapter 17. Needless to say, the major difficulties occur when you have had boarding school fees paid by your employer during the assignment and, with your child at a critical point in the run-up to major examinations, you are loath to move him or her to another cheaper or free school.

Accommodation

Getting back into your home or finding somewhere new to live can take weeks or months – and your furniture may be travelling across the oceans for just as long. You may need somewhere temporary to live until you can settle permanently. Many companies pay for this kind of accommodation, usually for up to four weeks with a further extension if you are having genuine difficulties finding anything suitable. If you are flexible on where you stay, they may agree to commute a month in a luxury hotel for a longer period in a short-lease apartment if the overall cost is not going to be any higher.

Some companies will pay for the legal fees associated with house purchase in the home location but this is the exception rather than the rule.

Customs duties

It can come as an unpleasant surprise if you have to pay customs duties on items purchased while overseas and you should be clear with your employer, before you depart for home, whether or not these charges will be reimbursed. Generally, they are not and duties on, for example, imported wines and spirits can be extremely high – a good reason for a large party before you leave the work location to finish off the booze left over from your stay. Most countries impose import duties on items which appear to have been purchased specifically for the purpose of importation at a lower cost than the prevailing rate in the home country. The main consideration is therefore the date of purchase, and it is worth keeping receipts of expensive items as evidence of how long they have been in your possession.

Resignation and redundancy

For many expatriates, the move back is not simply a matter of returning to the home country employer. What happens, for example, if you decide, before the end of the posting, that you cannot continue in the assignment or if your employer tells you that you are no longer required either in the work location or at the home base?

There are several reasons why you might want to curtail an assignment. Many are related to the additional stresses of expatriate life; there may also be domestic problems at home which force you to return. In these circumstances, your employer may be less flexible than you think, especially if the assignment is for a contracted period. An end of assignment bonus may have to be forfeited in some cases; in others, the degree of assistance with relocation costs could be restricted. As a general rule, if the reasons for your return are beyond your control, they will usually be sympathetic; but if you simply decide that you are not happy, and you cannot be persuaded to stay, you may find that you are paying to move yourself back.

This will almost certainly be the case if you decide to resign and join another company while overseas. Your current employer will, quite fairly, take the view that, since your new employer has lured you away, he should pay for your return. If you are seriously considering a move to another company in your home base, either leave it until you have moved back at the expense of your current employer or be sure to negotiate a relocation package as part of the new deal. A few employers pre-empt this tactic by insisting that you reimburse the company for your repatriation costs if you elect to resign within two years after your return.

If you have your employment terminated during your assignment for gross misconduct (stealing from the company, physically abusing a fellow employee etc), you can expect to receive the minimum amount of help with your return.

One of the most difficult situations to face is being made redundant while overseas. Not only must you come to terms with the emotional difficulties of losing your livelihood, but you are almost certainly away from the place in which you have the greatest opportunity to find another job quickly. Trying to organize the move home and face the problems of reverse culture shock on top of this can be intolerable.

Your position, in terms of job security (and, therefore, the degree to which you will be exposed to redundancy), must be carefully considered before you decide to take on an expatriate assignment. Few overseas appointments carry a contractual guarantee to a job on your return and this risk is usually valued in terms of the financial premium for taking the position in the first place. While most companies take the view that they would not have invested in the assignee if they had not believed that he would have long-term value back in the home base, situations can change rapidly and, while you are away from where all the decisions are being made, the memory of your name has a tendency to fade. This is a good reason for showing up at the office during home leave and making sure that those who will ultimately make the decision about your future remember who you are and what you would like to do when the posting ends. As far as assurances are concerned, however, the best you can expect is a promise that your employer will endeavour to place you in a suitable position when you come back.

With this in mind, redundancy is an ever-present reality – as it is for your home-based counterpart. As an international employee, however, you are usually in a more vulnerable position. If you feel that the severance terms offered are inadequate, your ability to do something about it is limited. Legal action in your home base or the work location may not be successful; neither jurisdiction will be keen to hear a case which involves a situation arising in another country or one which may require an employer from another country to be summonsed. The majority of claims relating to unfair dismissal or inadequate compensation are settled out of court, since neither party wants to face the cost of a protracted case based on a dubious legal situation.

Because it is still relatively rare, few companies have a detailed policy for redundant expatriates. The usual approach is either to take the redundancy practice of the employee's home country (especially when he remains an employee of the company in the home base and is seconded to the work location) or establish a general global norm such as one month's salary for each year of service. Some employers will be sensitive in the way they handle the employee in this situation (probably wisely, if they want other staff to feel some degree of comfort in accepting an expatriate post in the future). Extended notice periods and continuation of full expatriate terms, while the employee sorts out the problems of relocating and finding a new job, are reasonably common practices. Some companies also extend outplacement services and retraining schemes to redundant employees so that their chances of finding the best possible new job are greatly enhanced.

As an expatriate, you may, of course, discover that you enjoy living in a particular country so much that you find yourself evading suggestions that it might be time to move on. The time will come when your employer is unwilling to give you the best of both worlds: a generous expatriate package and the stability and comfort of a country which you have begun to call home.

Obviously, if you tell your employer about your long-term intentions, he may decide to take the expatriate terms away overnight. If you wait to be found out, there is a chance that a package will be offered to integrate you into the local compensation structure – possibly over a number of years. Apart from actual salary, this could involve a gradual decline in the amount your employer is willing to pay towards schooling and housing costs. More problematic will be the question of your pension rights and you may have to accept that participation in the work location scheme will become mandatory, though you should normally be able to arrange for your accumulated pension rights in your home base plan to be transferred to the scheme in the new permanent location.

While there have been some exceptions, it is unlikely that your employer will put you on international terms if you subsequently decide to return to the original home base. The normal view is that, by localizing in another country, you have simply added an extra home base rather than replaced the old one with the new.

Conclusion

Most expatriates and their families, when they leave home, are too excited by the prospect of their new life to give much thought to the problems of returning home a few years later. However, managing the home trip may be the hardest part of the whole expatriate experience. The financial side is important but emotional damage from the shock of 're-entry' is the real thing to guard against, especially if you are returning to uncertain career prospects. Perhaps all expatriates coming home have to go through withdrawal symptoms and, in most cases, time takes care of the problem. Keeping in touch with the home base and not getting out of touch in the expatriate location may be the best way of preparing yourself for the problem that will have to be faced one day. Like the astronaut, the journey up is going to be difficult but getting back is always the trickiest part!

25. Zen and the Expatriate

Even after the most meticulous preparations, reading every page of this book and ploughing through all those checklists, there will be times when you and your family go through periods of doubt and anxiety. If you don't, you will certainly be in the minority and maybe far too thick-skinned to make a good expatriate anyway.

Apart from the money, many of us feel that living overseas is an opportunity for personal growth – learning about new cultures, meeting new people and experiencing a new lifestyle. Inevitably, the challenges of a new location will sometimes escalate into a crisis for you or a member of your family. The trick is to prepare mentally for stress and anxiety but to avoid an overdose which will be debilitating. Loneliness, anger, frustration and bewilderment are all normal reactions for an expatriate from time to time. They are part of the personal growth cycle in response to the challenges of the new setting.

If general experience is anything to go by, you can expect to encounter a number of emotional stages which merge into each other. For each individual, one stage may, of course, be more acute than another and may last for a longer period.

Pre-move emotions

The first stage of a move overseas begins not when the moving van arrives but rather when the idea is first broached. However many positive factors can be found to justify a move, there will be negative emotions with which to cope. Grandparents may be left behind and will miss important milestones in the lives of grandchildren. Spouses may resign from jobs or abandon carefully built-up positions in the local community. Children will lose friends at school and feel insecure. The career decision may be far from clear cut and lead to agonies of indecision. Managing all these negative feelings does not mean ignoring them. You and your family, who may look at things very differently, will hold views that range from justifiable to wholly illogical. The best way to cope is to accept them as a reality so they can be dealt with overtly, even if everyone cannot be made completely happy or reassured about the outcome of the move.

Arrival

Arrival is usually a time of euphoria. The commitment is past, the move has been made. Everything at the new location is interesting and exciting. Each small step with the local language, food and culture is a triumph. And then the high begins to wear off. The noise gets worse, there are too many people, the food upsets your bodily functions – and every task seems impossibly difficult. You are overwhelmed by the strangeness of the new environment and feel inadequate. This period may occur in the first few weeks or may be postponed for a number of months, but it will occur in a greater or lesser degree of intensity. In this stage of adjustment, each family member expends extra energy mastering newness. There are fewer safety valves for tensions and many more demands. The expatriate family needs to marshal all its reserves of strength and patience if it is to make a successful adjustment.

The negative expatriate stage often manifests itself in irritated criticism of the local people. The moaning and carping do have a positive aspect as they make expatriates appreciate the reality of the community rather than some idealized version.

Feeling at home

Then, imperceptibly, the expatriate begins to feel comfortable with the local ways, understands the job and begins to feel part of the community. The family refer to 'back home' less frequently and a network of friends is established locally. The reasons why people do things the way they do become more evident. The attractions of the home base become less obvious, the bouts of homesickness less frequent. These are the rewards of personal development – more tolerance, a better understanding of an alien culture and, on reflection, a better appreciation of your own culture as well.

Of course, it doesn't always work like this. Some crises become too acute, some emotions too unmanageable and the expatriate and family have no choice but to head home. Others manage to stay on but only by wrapping themselves in a cocoon that isolates them from the local community. This happens to the minority. If you can realize, at the lowest point, that all the negative feelings are merely a natural part of adjustment, feeling at home will happen all the more speedily.

Boredom

An expat is a gypsy and the longer the lifestyle prevails the more ingrained become the instincts of the gypsy. After a year or maybe three, a vague sense of ennui may creep up on you. This does not mean that the assignment location is particularly boring – although, of course, it may be – but that it is time to move on. Changing locations every three years or so acts like a drug which becomes habit forming. New places, new experiences beckon and the desire to shed the old skin becomes stronger and stronger. Jobs and friends become boring, the local club looks tatty and the local politics seem more mind-numbing than usual. It is all the call of the road. Whether you succumb to this stage is a matter of personality and circumstance. If you do, your career will become a succession of overseas assignments and life stages will be remembered by where you were at the time. If you cling grimly to the original location, you earn the title of 'old hand' which does not always have complimentary connotations.

However it develops, it is probably fate or karma – you learn the inner game of being an expatriate – and you play the role allotted to you. Life is a journey and there is no finishing line!

Further Reading

Home and Away, a useful monthly newsletter (Expats International, 29 Lacon Road, London SE22 9HE)

Resident Abroad, a monthly publication (Financial Times Business Information, 102-108 Clerkenwell Road, London EC1M 5SA)

Nexus Expatriate Magazine, a monthly publication (Expat Network Ltd, Carolyn House, Dingwall Road, Croydon, Surrey CR0 9XF)

The Happy European: A Survival Guide to the EC, Laetitia de Warren (Charles Letts)

Books published by Kogan Page

Buying a Property in France: The Daily Telegraph Guide, 4th edition, Philip Jones, 1993

How to Get the Best Deal from Your Employer, Martin Edwards, 1991

Living and Retiring Abroad: The Daily Telegraph Guide, Michael Furnell, 6th edition, 1992

Portable Careers: How to Survive Your Partner's Relocation, Linda R Greenbury, 1992

Working Abroad: The Daily Telegraph Guide to Living and Retiring Abroad, Godfrey Golzen (annual)

Your Employment Rights, Michael Malone, 1992 (text applies to United Kingdom only)

Index of Advertisers

Index

The Expatriate's Handbook